YOUR KINGDOM COME

Your Kingdom Come

THE LORD'S PRAYER, NOT A LITURGY, NOT A MODEL PRAYER, BUT A WHOLE NEW WAY OF LIFE.

Howard Sands

Sands Rodway Trust

Copyright © 2021 by Howard Sands

All rights reserved. No part of this book may be reproduced in any manner whatsoever without written permission except in the case of brief quotations embodied in critical articles and reviews.

First Printing, 2022

© 2010-2020 These concepts were developed during the above years and preached at several churches in Australia and Africa during that time.

ISBN: 978-0-6453245-0-1
Cover design: Howard Sands
Photography: Howard Sands, Port Stephens, NSW, Australia
Proof reading: Tom Salter
Editorial comments and assistance: Dr Barry Chant

Scripture quotations as noted.

KJV - King James version, Public Domain
NKJV – New King James Version®. Copyright © 1982 by Thomas Nelson. Used by permission. All rights reserved.,
NIV – New International Version, The Holy Bible, New International Version, NIV Copyright 1973, 1978, 1984, 2011 by Biblica, Inc. Used by Permission. All rights reserved
CEV – Contemporary English Version, American Bible Society's (ABS) translation of the Contemporary English Version (CEV) that was first published in 1995, Used by Permission. All rights reserved
WEB – World English Bible, Public Domain
MSG - The Message Bible,   Scripture quotations marked MSG are taken from *THE MESSAGE*, copyright © 1993, 2002, 2018 by Eugene H. Peterson. Used by permission of NavPress. All rights reserved. Represented by Tyndale House Publishers, Inc.

Contents

Forward	1
Acknowledgements	**3**
1 Our Father	6
2 Which Art in Heaven, Hallowed be thy Name	26
3 Your Kingdom Come, Your Will be Done	38
4 Give us Today our Daily Bread	56
5 Forgive us our Debts	85
6 Lead us not into Temptation but Deliver us from Evil	101
7 The Doxology	126
Bibliography	139
What Australian Christian Leaders are saying	140
Other Books By Howard Sands	144
About The Author	147

Forward

Forward

"Your Kingdom Come". What a great title for a book I thought as I began reading Howard's manuscript. Knowing his powerful and inspiring missions passion I knew this would have grown out of many years of strong personal prayer. It is a very strong, honest and practical handbook that is brilliantly compiled and full of strong revelation that will take the reader's spiritual life to a new dimension. This is a strategic book of very real significance for these turbulent times."

Evangelist Tim Hall
Founder Tim Hall International Ministries Inc.
Dip T (Diploma in teaching), Doctor of Ministry.
46+ years in ministry and evangelism globally.

Acknowledgements

To my heavenly Father, you love me so much, to not only provide for my salvation through Jesus, but also bring me into your family, giving me your very DNA, calling me your son and making me like you. You called me righteous, something I could never achieve, and you brought me into a relationship that has brought forth this understanding of how you meant for us to live. Without you I am nothing.

To my wife Joy, thank you for standing by my side through 40 years of life with all its ups and downs, celebrations and disappointments, its successes and failures, raising a family, travelling the world, times of separation in missions, you are my best friend and without you none of this would have been possible. I love you so much.

To the people I learned under in my early years as a Christian, you taught me what it means to trust God, to have faith and proceed, to know that I am loved by God and righteous in His eyes. There are many, but special mention must go to Pastor Jean Pierre Reifler OAM, who led me to Jesus, brothers Pastors David and Robin Taylor, under whose ministry I learned so much in my early years.

To my Bible College principal Pastor Hal Oxley OBE (Lt Col Australian Army, WW2 veteran, Rats of Tobruk, Deputy Director Australian Military Intelligence, founder Life Ministry Church, Life Ministry Bible College and Oxley College, founder Associated Christian Ministries) and college dean Pastor Alan Vandenberg who cemented the word of God in my life.

To Apostles Cliff and Helen Beard, for inspiring faith, taking me on my first and second mission trips to India, along with Pastor Neil Milne, that set me on a path of missions I never saw coming that has now spanned over 42 years and seen me visit over 26 countries for mission on every continent.

To people who touched my life along the way with the new creation message of who we are in Christ or who mentored me in my early ministry days and further along, people like Pastor Roy Hullah, Pastor Peter Coles, Pastor Peter Allard, Ross Knight, Pastor Tony Ashdown, Pastor Martin Goodall, Pastor Keith Ainge, Pastor Eric Roggeveen.

To the many people who have stood alongside Joy and I in ministry as co-workers, supporters and members in Mildura, Wagga Wagga, Canberra, Penrith, Rouse Hill and St Marys.

To the many pastors who have been brave enough to invite me to their pulpit across Australia and across the world or prepare events for us to minister at; from crusades large and small, leadership trainings, church planting seminars and unity seminars, we whole heartedly thank you. A special thanks must go to Indian Pastors VA & Mrs Mariamma Thampy and sons Biju and Binu, Rev Dr Henry Joseph (late) and his sons Rev Dr Charles Finny Joseph and

Rev Dr Alex Joseph, Dr PG Vargis who I have had the privilege of working with extensively in many parts of India for decades..

To those wordsmiths skilled in sentence construction, grammar etc that have commented on and helped edit this work, thank you, especially Tom Salter and Rev Dr Barry Chant.

Without these people in my life, I never would have come to the sweet fellowship I enjoy with my saviour Jesus and be able to share the deep truths of His love with you. My deepest thanks.

1

Our Father

The Lord's Prayer is often spoken aloud in churches and at religious events, I wonder if we have ever thought much about what we are praying, or is it just a thing we do? What does God think about our tritely saying our prayer without any thought to the content let alone how it might challenge or change our lives or our relationship to Him?

Consider this drama presentation.

A person is saying their prayers, saying the Lord's Prayer, when God interrupts them.

Person: "Our Father which art in heaven..."
God: Yes?

Person: Don't interrupt me. I'm praying.
God: But you called me!

Person: Called you? I didn't call you. I'm praying. "Our Father which art in heaven..."
God: There, you did it again.

Person: Did what?

God: Called me. You said, "Our Father which art in heaven." Here I am...what's on your mind?

Person: But I didn't mean anything by it. I was, you know, just saying my prayers for the day. I always say the Lord's Prayer. It makes me feel good, kind of like getting a duty done.

God: All right. Go on.

Person: Hallowed be thy name..."

God: Hold it. What do you mean by that?

Person: By what?

God: By "hallowed be thy name"?

Person: It means...it means...good grief, I don't know what it means. How should I know? It's just a part of the prayer. By the way, what does it mean?

God: It means honored, holy, wonderful.

Person: Hey, that makes sense. I never thought about what "hallowed" meant before. "Thy kingdom come, thy will be done, on earth as it is in heaven."

God: Do you really mean that?

Person: Sure, why not?

God: What are you doing about it?

Person: Doing? Nothing, I guess. I just think it would be kind of neat if you got control of everything down here like you have up there.

God: Have I got control of you?

Person: Well, I go to church.

God: That isn't what I asked you. What about your bad temper? You've really got a problem there, you know. And then there's the way you spend your money--all on yourself. And what about the kind of books you read?

Person: Stop picking on me! I'm just as good as some of the rest of those people at the church.

God: Excuse me. I thought you were praying for my will to be done. If that is to happen, it will have to start with the ones who are praying for it. Like you, for example.

Person: Oh, all right. I guess I do have some hang-ups. Now that you mention it, I could probably name some others.

God: So, could I.

Person: I haven't thought about it very much until now, but I really would like to cut out some of those things. I would like to, you know, be really free.

God: Good. Now we're getting somewhere. We'll work together, you and I. Some victories can truly be won. I'm proud of you.

Person: Look, Lord, I need to finish up here. This is taking a lot longer than it usually does. "Give us this day, our daily bread."

God: You need to cut out the bread. You're overweight as it is.

Person: Hey, wait a minute? What is this, "Criticize me day"? Here I was doing my religious duty and all of a sudden you break in and remind me of all my hang-ups.

God: Praying is a dangerous thing. You could wind up changed, you know. That's what I'm trying to get across to you. You called me, and here I am. It's too late to stop now. Keep praying, I'm interested in the next part of your prayer. (Pause). Well, go on.

Person: I'm scared to.

God: Scared? Of what?

Person: I know what you'll say.

God: Try me and see.

Person: "Forgive us our sins, as we forgive those who sin against us."

God: What about Ann?

Person: See? I knew it! I knew you would bring her up! Why Lord, she's told lies about me, spread stories about my family. She never paid back the debt she owes me. I've sworn to get even with her!

God: *But, your prayer? What about your prayer?*

Person: I didn't mean it.

God: *Well, at least you're honest. But it's not much fun carrying that load of bitterness around inside, is it?*

Person: No, but I'll feel better as soon as I get even. Boy, have I got some plans for that neighbour. She'll wish she had never moved into this neighbourhood.

God: *You won't feel any better. You'll feel worse. Revenge isn't sweet. Think of how unhappy you already are, but I can change all that.*

Person: You can? How?

God: *Forgive Ann. Then I'll forgive you. Then the hate and sin will be Ann's problem and not yours. You will have settled your heart.*

Person: Oh, you're right, You always are, and more than I want to revenge Ann, I want to be right with you. (pause)...(sigh). All right. All right. I forgive her. Help her to find the right road in life, Lord. She's bound to be awfully miserable now that I think about it. Anybody who goes around doing the things she does to others has to be out of it. Someway, somehow, show her the right way.

God: *There now! Wonderful! How do you feel?*

Person: Hmmmmmmm. Well, not bad. Not bad at all. In fact, I feel pretty great! You know, I don't think I'll have to go to bed uptight tonight for the first time since I can remember. Maybe I won't be so tired from now on because I'm not getting enough rest.

God: *You're not through with your prayer. Go on...*

Person: Oh, all right. "And lead us not into temptation, but deliver us from evil."

God: *Good! Good! I'll do that. Just don't put yourself in a place where you can be tempted.*

Person: What do you mean by that?

God: Don't turn on the TV when you know the laundry needs to be done and the house needs to be picked up. Also, about the time you spend coffeeing with your friends, if you can't influence the conversation to positive things, perhaps you should rethink the value of those friend-ships. Another thing, your neighbours and friends shouldn't be your standard for "keeping up". And please don't use me for an escape hatch.

Person: I don't understand the last part.

God: Sure you do. You've done it a lot of times. You get caught in a bad situation. You get into trouble and then you come running to me, "Lord, help me out of this mess, and I promise you I'll never do it again." You remember some of those bargains you tried to make with me?

Person: Yes, and I'm ashamed, Lord. I really am.

God: Which bargain are you remembering?

Person: Well, there was the night that Bill was gone and the children and I were home alone. The wind was blowing so hard I thought the roof would go any minute and tornado warnings were out. I remember praying, "Oh God, if you'll spare us, I'll never skip my devotions again."

God: I protected you, but you didn't keep your promise, did you?

Person: I'm sorry, Lord, I really am. Up until now I thought that if I just prayed the Lord's Prayer every day, then I could do what I liked. I didn't expect anything to happen like it did.

God: Go ahead and finish your prayer.

Person: "For Thine is the kingdom, and the power, and the glory forever." Amen.

God: Do you know what would bring me glory? What would really make me happy?

Person: No, but I'd like to know. I want now to please you. I can see what a mess I've made of my life, and I can see how great it would be to really be one of your followers.

God: You just answered the question.

Person: I did?

God: Yes. The thing that would bring me glory is to have people like you truly love me, and I see that happening between us. Now that some of these old sins are exposed and out of the way, well, there is no telling what we can do together!

©1977 Author: Clyde Lee Herring, 2938 East 84th St., Tulsa, OK 74137

Numerous attempts through various channels have been made to contact the author and his publisher for permission but no response has been received.

Praise the Lord! You've probably read the Lord's Prayer. You've probably prayed the Lord's Prayer. Did you ever pray it like that, with interruptions?

Let us read Matthew 6:8-10. There are two versions of the Lord's Prayer in the scriptures. One version says,

Be not ye therefore like unto them: for your Father knoweth what things ye have need of, before ye ask him. After this manner therefore pray ye: Our Father which art in heaven, hallowed be thy name. Thy kingdom come, Thy will be done in earth, as it is in heaven. KJV

You will also find it in Luke 11:1-4

And it came to pass, that, as he was praying in a certain place, when he ceased, one of his disciples said unto him, Lord, teach us to pray, as John also taught his disciples. And he said unto them, When ye pray, say, Our Father which art in heaven, Hallowed be thy name. Thy kingdom come. Thy will be done, as in heaven, so in earth. Give us day by day our daily bread. And forgive us our sins; for we also forgive every one that is indebted to us. And lead us not into temptation; but deliver us from evil. KJV

Let's pray together.

Father, we thank you that you've shown us how to pray and Father, we ask you to help us to learn not just about prayer but what you're teaching us through this prayer. Father we thank you for the anointing of your Spirit, to open our ears and our eyes to see things in your word today. In Jesus' name, amen.

How important is it that we pray?

How much do you pray? Do you pray more than an hour a day?

Do you pray more than half an hour a day?

Do you pray more than five minutes a day?

Do you pray sometimes?

Or do you pray occasionally when you think about it?

I think that what Jesus was actually teaching us was not that we should pray and repeat the words he had given us; although in the two versions, which seemingly are on two different occasions, he said almost the same words, but he was teaching us something about life. The first verse in Matthew chapter 6 is part of the Sermon on the Mount.

The Lord's Prayer is part of Jesus' teaching on life. It is part of the Sermon on the Mount, which is not a teaching on prayer, it's a teaching on character and behaviour and how to live, and within this sermon, the Lord's Prayer teaches us how we ought to conduct our relationship with God.

In Luke chapter 11, Jesus is teaching the disciples in answer to their questions "Teach us how to pray". I don't think he's giving them a model prayer as much as he's giving them a teaching on prayer.

The whole of the gospel message is wrapped up in this short prayer. So, I'm going to gradually unpack this prayer. I think there's a lot of value for our lives in it.

I want us to see, that in this prayer is the whole of the gospel message and how it is relevant to every aspect of our lives. This is the entire gospel message wrapped up and encased in these few words. This is relevant not only to prayer, but to every aspect of our lives.

First of all, a little bit of history. The Lord's Prayer, the text, as we know it, as you read it at the start with God's interruptions, comes from a decision that was taken by the church in England in the 1500s when English was gradually starting to replace Latin in the church.

It was in 1541 that the bishops met and decided on a form of prayer for the Lord's Prayer in English. Now it was only then – we're talking what? A little under five hundred years ago. It's not that long. It's 1500 plus years after Christ before it became known in a common language. That's pretty amazing really.

However this form of the Lord's Prayer, adopted at the time and following most closely to the Tyndale translation of the Bible, was adopted into the Book of Common Prayer in 1549 just eight years after they decided on the format, and yet back in 1519 not so many years earlier, seven people were martyred, burnt at the stake in Coventry for teaching their children the Ten Commandments and the Lord's Prayer in English.

From 1519 through to 1546, there was a radical change and shift in the thinking of the church. It was illegal to use the English language for the liturgies of the Ten Commandments and the Lord's Prayer, the perpetrators found guilty of this great horror for teaching them to their children in English were burned at the stake. But this radical change saw the Lord's Prayer being adopted as the form of prayer for the church in England. [The separating of the Catholic Church into the Church of England and subsequent Protestant denominations had formally begun in 1534 with King Henry V111's renouncing of papal authority with the first Act of Supremacy in 1534. This was repealed by subsequent Monarch Queen Mary 1, until it was re-enacted as the second act of supremacy under the reign of Queen Elizabeth 1 in 1558.] It is clear it was a time of great turmoil in Christendom during this period, with the age of reformation also taking hold of Europe.

This had created a great shift. Now there had been English versions of the Lord's Prayer for a long time before that. In fact, the earliest recorded English version of the Lord's Prayer was the Northumbrian version dated about 650 AD. So nearly a thousand years earlier there was a known English version. Yet the version we are familiar with came into being in 1549 in the Book of Common Prayer.

The later versions of the scriptures, which came out shortly after that, the Rheims Version of 1581 and the King James Version in 1611, have variations to the text but basically follow the same wording.

That version has now been uniformly taught throughout the English-speaking world for almost five hundred years and except for a few modern revisions of it, it has remained pretty much the same. I was at a church recently and they said the Lord's Prayer. It was a Korean church where I was speaking and they said the English version of the Lord's Prayer in a modern translation that I found hard to follow, because I hadn't heard it before. Yet I suppose that most of us have learned the Lord's Prayer in our younger days and the majority of us would say pretty much the same words.

Our purpose in looking at this prayer.
Many different churches have taught many different things about the Lord's Prayer over the years and our purpose is not to look at the how and the why of a liturgy, which it has been used as, but more at what Christ was teaching about life in this prayer.

Frankly, I am not that interested in the liturgy. Don't get me wrong. I am interested, but not interested in the 'pie in the sky when I die'. I would rather have the steak on the plate while I wait!

I want to know how God is going to impact my life here and now. I know that there's heaven later, but I'm not in a hurry to go there; and I don't see many others in a hurry to get there either.

What I want to know is; what is God actually saying to me now and how is that going to affect my life here on earth? And how is my life going to be affected by what He's teaching me about prayer?

How did Jesus teach the Lord's Prayer? I've mentioned that there were two occasions, the Sermon on the Mount and in answer to the disciples' request. There are slight variations, but it seems very similar for the two occasions.

Therefore, it seems to be likely that Jesus is teaching on the way to approach prayer rather than a liturgy to be repeated. It's more of an instruction on what prayer is than a prayer to be repeated. Now if you decide to pray the prayer, pray the prayer as we did in our little example earlier, be prepared to let God interrupt you.

Don't be in a hurry to get through it because maybe when you say, "Our Father," you have addressed Him, and he may address you back and he may challenge you about some of the things that you're praying about. He may ask you to consider some of those things that perhaps we would just race through instead of thinking about what it is we are actually saying.

Jesus taught that vain repetition of prayer was something the heathen do. Matthew 6:7 He gave them this instruction just before He gave them the teaching called the Lord's Prayer. It's not something just to say and not think about. In fact, not just this prayer but any prayer is not a prayer to pray and not think about. If we're going to pray, then we ought to think about what it is that we pray.

Let's take the first words, the opening words. 'Our Father which art in heaven'. Did you notice in our example that the person praying didn't get very far before God interrupted? 'Our Father,' 'Oh, yes, here I am! You called me.' Jesus revealed God to people when he walked on the earth. God, Yahweh, Jehovah, Elohim, many names for God. In fact, probably about sixteen different names that the Jews had for God, but they didn't know him as Father, they knew him as God the Almighty, God the Creator, God to be Revered, God who was awesome. But they didn't know Him as Father.

He had revealed himself to them. He had shown his love and compassion and at different times throughout history, different people caught glimpses and little understandings of his Father heart though He has always had the Father heart, generally they didn't get it.

What we find through the history of God dealing with men and then through his chosen race, the Hebrews, is that, because they thought God was too awe-inspiring, too majestic to have any relationship with individuals, God instituted the priesthood so they could come close to him via the intermediary of a priest, this was God's method of relating to mankind until his perfect plan was put into place to bring mankind into close communion and direct relationship with Himself through his indwelling Son, Jesus Christ. Thus, the idea developed among the Hebrews that God was untouchable, unapproachable and unknowable because he was so awesome, just, powerful and holy, that He couldn't be approached by mere men, so they were continually reminded that they were evil and couldn't draw near to God. Therefore, the priesthood became their escapism from being directly relational with God. Although God called them back time and time again to relate directly to him, this did not occur until the New Testament (with a few prophetic exceptions), when Christ came to live in the believer and established a direct God to mankind relationship. "Christ in you, the hope of glory," Colossians 1:27 NIV; "And you also were included in Christ when you heard the message of truth, the gospel of your salvation. When you believed, you were marked in Him with a seal, the promised Holy Spirit." Ephesians 1:13 NIV

Therefore, the priesthood became the stumbling block preventing the people of God from understanding the Father's heart. They took the opinion that they were not holy enough, because of their sin, to approach God directly; therefore, they used the priest as an intermediary so that he could pray to God for them. This misconception has continued to this present day in much of our religious ideology. That misconception still prevents people from coming to God in their sinful state because they think they are unworthy and unacceptable to God and He is therefore unapproachable, but they couldn't be more wrong, they are ignorant of his promises. Jesus said, "All those the Father gives me will come to me, and whoever comes to me I will never drive away." John 6:37 NIV. King David said, "He has removed our sins as far from us as the east is from the west." Psalm 103:12 NLT. Apostle Peter said, "As a result, you have obeyed him and have been cleansed by the blood of Jesus Christ." 1 Peter 1:2 NLT. Apostle Paul said, "God made him who had no sin to be sin for us, so that in him we might become the righteousness of God." 2 Corinthians 5:21 NIV.

You understand that concept from the Old Testament. Now think about this. That concept is still alive and well in a lot of Christendom. We think that we are not worthy of coming into the presence of God. Therefore, we must have someone else to do that for us. One of the things that happens to me very often, especially when I'm in a foreign country, people will come and they will say, "Please pray for me for ..." Please pray for my family. Please pray for my children. Please pray for their school. Please pray for my daughter to have a baby. Please pray for this. Please pray for that.

Please pray for something else, as though I had somehow got more connection with God than they have.

No, I don't have any more connection to God than the next Christian, I have just realised the connection that I have with my Father and they perhaps haven't realised. You see the connection is that God made us his sons and daughters. He made us his children; therefore, He must be our Father. If he is our Father, then we can go to our Father. It's great that you can pray for somebody because they asked you to pray for them but we don't need someone to pray for us. We need to know that we have access ourselves.

It's great that we should pray for each other, the Bible encourages us to do that. It says, "For where two or three are gathered together in my name, there am I in the midst of them" Matthew 18:20 KJV. "Is any sick among you? Let him call for the elders of the church; and let them pray over him, anointing him with oil in the name of the Lord: And the prayer of faith shall save the sick, and the Lord shall raise him up; and if he have committed sins, they shall be forgiven him." James 5:14-15 KJV.

It tells us to do that. But we need to understand that we have access to our Father. When my children come over to our place (my two children are both married, have their own homes and have started their own families), they don't ask my permission to get something from the fridge, they just go there and get it as though it's theirs, because it is.

Jesus taught us about a relationship. He taught about the new birth. He said to Nicodemus, "... unless one is born anew, he cannot see God's kingdom". John 3:3 WEB I'm sure you've heard that story and that message many times, but what he was saying to Nicodemus was, 'you need to start over'. You need to start a different kind of relationship with God. You need to start one that's not based on the premise that you can't approach God. You need to get born into his family, so that you understand the closeness of the relationship, so that you understand the father-son connection.

If you're not born into his family, you will always seem like you're an outsider and you will always need a priest. You will always need someone to be an advocate between you and God; but God has not intended it to be that way. He has intended that you have your own access and that you come as a child comes to his father.

It's a radically different concept to what the Jews had. The relationship with God the Jews had at the time did not embrace that, even though God in his efforts and his dealings with mankind for hundreds and hundreds of years had tried to convince them and convey that to them.

Jesus said, "Come unto me all you that labour and are heavy burdened and I will give you rest." Matthew 11:28, WEB repeating the words of God to Moses in Exodus 33:14 when he had just delivered the children of Israel from Egypt.

This had always been God's intention and heart but because of their hard heart they had not been able to receive Him that way.

When the young David consoled himself in the Lord, because King Saul was pursuing him, he talked about his relationship with God. Psalm 18

It had always been God's intention and heart to have a relationship with his special people, but because of their hard heart they had not been able to receive him that way. Jesus taught the value of mankind, that they were precious in God's eyes, like a child is to its father. He said, "You are worth more than many sparrows." Matthew 10:31 CEV

"Jesus said, "Let the little children come to me, and do not hinder them, for the kingdom of heaven belongs to such as these." Matthew 19:14; Mark 10:14; Luke 18:16 NIV

Jesus taught that we could come to His Father. The notion that God is far removed and above approach by mere humans was a contrary thought to what God wanted his children to have of Him, God had always wanted to have a relationship with his chosen people.

The prophets tried to convince people that they could have a relationship with God, and yet the people didn't get it. Ezekiel prophesied that, "A new heart also will I give you, and a new spirit will I put within you: and I will take away the stony heart out of your flesh, and I will give you an heart of flesh". Ezekiel 36:26 KJV They didn't get it because they were living by head knowledge and not by revelation. It is just the same today.

People, who knew they were sinners (breakers of God's law) taught that all were not worthy of approaching God and so it was ingrained into people that they should have a mediator between them and God, someone able to touch and feel them, but holy and able to relate to God. This was the purpose of the priesthood, but even their priests failed too and needed to make regular sacrifices.

Jesus has now reversed the concept of priesthood and given full access to the Father to all who have created a relationship with Him.

Jesus spoke about his relationship with God as his Father. In fact, if anything, that is probably the thing that angered the Jewish religious leaders the most. That he spoke about God as his Father; that he spoke about having a relationship with God. The Jewish leaders had made it religious, and Jesus messed with their religious practice (and the need for priests), this was probably the biggest contributing factor to the reason they wanted to kill him and get rid of him.

They couldn't understand that a person could have a relationship with God as Jesus had with his Father. They couldn't understand that Jesus could be God or the Son of God. They didn't understand. It implies a close personal nature of the relationship between God and those praying, like the father and the child.

Jesus taught about having a close relationship with God throughout his whole ministry, but he didn't teach it just as a new teaching, He wanted us to embrace it. You can believe something, (give mental assent to it) saying "I understand it, I believe it," but not act on it; often the church has taken hold of something and said, "This is what we believe," but still doesn't do it. This is not what Jesus taught, as with His example of the parable of the two sons whom their father asked to go and work in his vineyard, one said he would, but didn't; the other said he wouldn't but later repented and did. Matthew 21:28-32 James also says, Do not merely listen to the word, and so deceive yourselves. Do what it says. James 1:22 NIV.

I often say, "I can see your faith. You wear your faith on your shirt sleeves." You do. You wear it on your shirt sleeves. You can see my faith by what I do, by the way I live. What do I believe? I do what I believe. If I say I believe something, but don't do it, I don't really believe it. I just have it as a mental assent. But if I have belief,

I've taken it and I've embraced it and it has become mine and it's what I live... I live it out.

So, if I say that I believe God will answer a prayer, then I will pray with believing faith. I will pray with a matter of fact that God is able to both hear and answer and will answer my prayer. I will pray with such a passion. I will pray with such conviction. I will pray with such faith, expecting, fully expecting that God will hear me and answer me.

I will then take my actions and start living as though he has already answered me before I yet see it, because that's what I believe. I believe what I'm actually doing. Jesus was teaching that we come to God as a child comes to his father, a loving father who gives access and gives his children good things. God's heart has always been this way but throughout the Old Testament time, and even today, many did not receive Him this way. They did not receive his love, his heart, his intention, to be a Father.

Jesus taught the value of mankind; that they were precious in God's eyes. This is why we generally think in our society that people should be preserved. This is why we think that babies should not be aborted. This is why we think that we shouldn't kill off our old people saying they're no longer useful to society. This is why we believe that people have value. However, so much of our society has started to degenerate and these values are starting to fall.

But God has put value on people. He has put value on us because we are his sons and his daughters therefore you have value. Just think about this, if your father was somebody really, really, really – (did I mention really?) really important, you would grow up with a sense of importance. Isn't that true?

Do you think Prince William, the Duke of Cambridge (son of Prince Charles and Princess Dianna of UK) has a sense of his own worthiness, of his own importance? Brought up as the heir – number two in line to the throne, do you think he has a feeling of "I'm somebody"?

He might not prance it around, but he has it. He knows his purpose in life; that one day he will be king. He has that sense of purpose, and now as a young man, it's starting to show in his actions. He's starting to take on a regal kind of "hey, I'm here. I'm cool. But I'm important" air.

Now if your father was somebody really, really, really, really, really important, you would have that sense of importance, wouldn't you? Instead of that we think of our background, we think of our childhood, we think of our upbringing, we think of our job, we think of our wealth or lack thereof and we think, "I'm not important."

It has nothing to do with any of that. You see, we have been brought into a family where our Father is really, really, really important. He's actually the creator of the universe and he said, "You are my special daughter, you are my special son, you are the special one. You're the apple of my eye. You're the one that I adore. You're the one that I'm doting on. You're the one that I want to do special things with. You're the one. You. You. You. You. I want to do special things with you."

Does that change the way we think about God? Does that change the way we pray? Does that change the way we act in our life? Absolutely it does. Our Father, wow! Jesus taught that we could come to this Father. The notion that God is far removed and above approach by mere humans is contrary to what God wanted to teach his people. God had always wanted to have a relationship with his chosen people. People who knew that they were sinners, breakers of God's law, taught that such people were not worthy of approaching God. Therefore, it was ingrained into everyone that they should have a mediator between themselves and God, someone to touch and feel them, but totally holy and able to relate with God.

That was the purpose of the priesthood because people couldn't see that they could actually touch God themselves.

All right. Now we have started our prayer.

"Our Father" We now know who our Father is.

2

Which Art in Heaven, Hallowed be thy Name

"Which art in heaven" Jesus was bridging the unbridgeable in this sentence. "Which art in heaven." There's a gap between earth where I am and heaven where He is.

I think I cannot go there and those from there cannot come here or maybe they can, but we can't recognise them if they do. I can't go to heaven. It's too far away. It's too inaccessible, but Jesus came and said, "I'm from heaven. I've bridged the gap." Now it's accessible. Heaven is accessible. The one that we thought was unapproachable, the God in heaven, is not. Heaven and earth are not really far apart. The gap is bridgeable.

In fact, it's interesting.....I wonder where heaven is. You can draw a map of the world and you can locate the land masses and the countries and the seas. Name the seas. You can draw a map a bit bigger, a map of the solar system and there's the sun and there's

Mercury and Venus and Earth, Mars, all the planets. You can draw a map of the entire universe. There are millions of stars, most of which have not been named by us. God named them. But there is nowhere on your map that says heaven, is there? We've not pinpointed it down and said, "There it is!" Now actually, if heaven was on earth, I think it would be in the South of India. I think it would be in Kerala, sorry, but it's such a beautiful place. Or it might be some other place. It might be in Port Douglas in north Queensland, Australia which is very nice too.

Where is heaven? If it's not on the map, where is it? I think heaven is here. It's in a different dimension that we have not yet really learned how to touch. When we start to come to God, we start to touch heaven. When we start to realise that we can talk to our heavenly Father; we can talk to him and he can talk back to us, maybe heaven is here. Maybe heaven is just such a different dimension that our mind cannot grasp it.

Heaven is not far away. At times people say, "Oh, I tried to pray but the heavens were as brass," or "I tried to pray and my prayers didn't go any higher than the ceiling." Well maybe your prayers don't need to go any higher than the ceiling. Maybe your prayers just need to be heartfelt and full of faith because God is right here and he hears us when we pray.

I think that heaven is in the understanding of the relationship that we have with God the Father and that we have come into that relationship. We have been, as Jesus put it, 'born again'. We have become his sons by asking him into our life. We have taken that step of saying, "Yes, God. I want a relationship with you. I acknowledge that I'm a sinner. I acknowledge that I don't have the capacity to come to you, but I ask you to forgive me, cleanse me, and come into my life." If you do that, He will be forever connected to you.

Now, you can come to the front of a meeting. You can say a sinner's prayer, or you can say it in your heart. It doesn't matter. I said it over a little wrought iron table about two feet across in the backyard of somebody's house.

Where you make your commitment to God doesn't matter. How you say it doesn't matter. What you feel in your heart matters, that you make a commitment of your life to God. Not that I'm just going to turn over a new leaf, but that I'm going to invite him into my life. Jesus said, "You must be born again". You must. He didn't say it's a good idea, it's a good option, it's one of the better ones. No, he said you MUST be born again. You must be – he said, "I am the way, the truth and the life. No one comes to the Father except by me".

Sorry. Buddha won't take you there. Muhammad won't take you there. Confucius won't take you there. They've just got teaching about life, which doesn't take you to heaven. Jesus is the only one of all the great religious leaders of the world that ever said, "I am the only way." It must be pretty important then. He said, I am the only way. Let's come to him.

"Hallowed be thy name".
"Our Father, which art in heaven, hallowed be thy name." What on earth does that mean? The definition of "hallowed" according to the dictionary is; sanctified, consecrated, highly venerated, sacrosanct. Hallowed.

To hallow is to make or to set apart as holy. Something that is holy. It's not for the normal purpose. It's not for everyday use. It's holy. It's special. My mum has a special dinnerware set in the cupboard. Not the cupboard where we get the dishes for everyday use. She has the special dinner set, the fancy gold leaf-edged plates in their own cupboard. Maybe you also have special crockery that comes out for special occasions.

Well, hallowed means we've set that apart as special and it only comes out for special occasions. We've hallowed the dinner set. The plates have been set apart and we've hallowed them. We've set them apart as special and that's what we are doing with His name. Hallowed be thy name. We are setting it apart as special. Why would we do that? Because we need to give it the respect that it deserves. We need to give the name some means of separating it from the every day. The name of God, including the name of Jesus.

Although God is approachable and loving and caring; we're not to become too complacent, forgetting his awesomeness – I love that word. Awesomeness. He's awesome. I want you to think about the power of God for a minute, the power – the awesome, the majestic, the grandiose power of God. Just for a moment, think of the universe. Massive, massive, massive, huge, huge, massive. One tiny spec over there is called Earth, right?

Think for a moment about the raging bushfires. Think about the raging storms on the ocean. I'm sure you've seen some movie about some great storm on the ocean, somebody maybe losing their life or some ship going down (Titanic). The magnificence of that iceberg. Just think about the size of the volcanoes and the power when they erupt on the earth. Think about earthquakes. We've had a few. Think about the power of the earthquakes. Think about the power that's inherent in the earth. Just the storms and the wind. Amazing. Mankind builds these great edifices and God goes, "Poof!" and it's gone because that's the power of God.

Mankind's greatness is nothing. We need to respect God as holy. We need to understand and respect Him as the powerful creator, the one of unsearchable riches. We need to respect his power. We need to respect his name. His name is above every name and at the name of Jesus, every knee will bow. There's something about the name.

First, we need to understand that the Jews had a different custom to what we do in the western world in the naming of their children. When they named their children, they gave them a name that was to define them. Their name spoke about their purpose in life. It even spoke about their character.

You remember some stories in the Old Testament, how God said, "I'm going to change your name." He changed their name because he was giving them a new character. He was bringing forth out of them some new character.

Abram was changed to Abraham. Jacob was changed to Israel. Sarai was changed to Sarah. God said a name is important. A name is important and people's names were bound up with their character and who they were and their purpose and their destiny in life. So, it's not just, oh, I like Kylie. That's all right for a name. Nowadays we often choose names just because we like them.

No, in the Old Testament in the Jewish tradition, a name defined a person. So, when the Jews had this understanding about a name and Jesus said, "When you pray say...hallowed be thy name." Think about the name. Think about the name. Hallow it. Set it apart. Sanctify it. Treat it as special, but why? Why isn't it just about God? Why is it about the name? We could sanctify God and say, "Well, God is special. God is set apart", but he says, "Hallowed be thy name," not hallowed be thou. Why is that? Because the name speaks about the person. The person and the name are synonymous.

I am Howard. When you talk about Howard, you talk about me, whether you say good things or not, you talk about me. That's who I am. When you talk with someone else and you mention Howard, they think of me because I'm synonymous with my name. It's not just my label. It's who I am. Your name is who you are.

When the Jews named their children, they named them with purpose, to forge their destiny, to forge their purpose in life. God is holy and his name is holy because his name is HIM. If he is holy, his name is holy. He tells us, when we pray, let's pray to this God, who we now know, whom we have a relationship with as Father. We now know that he is hallowed, he is separated, he's awesome in power and majesty, but so is his name. Jesus helped us to understand the power of his name. He said, "Until now, you have not asked for anything in my name. Ask and you will receive and your joy will be complete." John 16:24 NIV.

Whatever you ask in His name, the Father will give it to you. The prayer is in His name, because we're invoking the person that the name speaks of. So, when I pray, I don't just pray and say, "Thank you for this and thank you for that. I will receive this and I will receive that," but "I thank you Father that in Jesus' name, because you said that I could have it, I can receive this."

I can use the name as the authority to take it. It belongs to me because the name has been given to me. Jesus said, "Until now you have not asked for anything in my name. Ask and you will receive, and your joy will be complete." John 16:24 NIV In other words, "You've not asked anything in my name, so you haven't got it. Therefore, ask in my name, so that you can receive it."

In Acts 4:12 NIV it says, "Salvation is found in no one else, for there is no other name under heaven given to mankind by which we must be saved." No other name. How important is the name? By invoking the name, we invoke the power behind the name. We invoke the person of the name.

I'm hoping that this will help you in prayer, so when you pray you can go to your heavenly Father, who you now have access to, whom you now understand in a loving Father-son relationship and you know how, in spite of how hallowed, holy and separate he is, he has given you access to himself. Wow! That's just amazing.

Then you can come to Him and you can ask something in his name because he said to you, "Use my name." Jesus said, "Use my name." For example, if you are looking for a job and somebody says to you, "Go to these people and say blah, blah, blah, has sent you." That's using their name. We call it name-dropping.

We are using their name to go to somebody and say so and so said that I should come and see you. We're using the name. Jesus said, "Use the name. The name has power. The name ..."

You see Jesus said that we can use his name because the Father has given him everything, everything. Everything. Can you say everything? Everything. Some can't say that. Everything! Because it is too high for their mind to believe that they have everything, not because they cannot believe it, but because of the impoverished thinking they have been taught and trained to have; that by thinking such things, they will put themselves on too high a pedestal.

Jesus said, "I've made it available to you. I've made it available to you. But you've got to use my name. It's not a formula. You have a relationship with me. Therefore, I have given it to you. Therefore, go and exercise the authority that I have given to you. I have given to you authority to use my name. Everything is subject to my name. Every knee will bow to my name. Everything is available in my name. I created it all anyway." He's given you the name to use, the name has ALL authority.

So, when we pray, we don't pray as I've heard people pray, like this. "Father, if it be your will, let such and such happen." Essentially Jesus said, 'Pray in my name. Ask in my name. Call things that be not, as though they were as Abraham did. Speak things into being as though you were the one that created the world, because the one who created the world is in you.'

Wow, that's a pretty radical thought, isn't it? The one who created the world is in you – or is he? Or is he? Have you asked Him in? Have you asked Him to come into your life? Have you asked Him to take up residency? Have you asked Him to cleanse you and forgive you and come in and make you born again? Have you become a person who has a father-son relationship with the heavenly Father?

Why do you think the devil wants to destroy the name of Jesus? Why do you think that the name of Jesus is a common swear word? You don't go out on a building site and hear some guy hammering a nail, hitting his thumb by accident and saying, "Oh, Buddha!" It doesn't happen.

He says, "Jesus!" doesn't he? Why? He's not calling upon the name of Jesus. He's letting out an expletive because he's in pain. Why is the name of Jesus dragged through the dirt? The name of Jesus is higher than any other name. Why should we allow it to be dragged through the dirt? But the reason is the devil wants to make it common. He wants to make it of low value. He wants us to not realise that there is power in that name, by making it common, by making it worthless. Then we will not realise the power that is associated with that name and others who don't know Him will not know that there is power in that name because it's something common. There's no respect for the name. When there's no respect for the name, there's no respect for the person behind the name.

A friend of mine, Pastor Roy Hullah, was a plasterer and he used to go out on the building sites and he would hear people using the name of the Lord in vain. He said to me many times, "I just go up to them and say, 'You're talking about my Lord and Saviour. Would you like to rephrase that?" because he wanted them to know the importance of the name.

Philippians 2:10 NIV says, "that **at the name of Jesus every knee should bow**, in heaven and on earth and under the earth", 1 John 3:23 NIV says, "And this is his command: **to believe in the name of his Son, Jesus Christ,** and to love one another as he commanded us."

Colossians 3:17 NIV says, "And whatever you do, whether in word or deed, **do it all in the name of the Lord Jesus**, giving thanks to God the Father through him."

There's a song we sometimes sing.

> My hope is built on nothing less
> Than Jesus' blood and righteousness
> I dare not trust the sweetest frame
> **But wholly trust in Jesus' name**
>
> *Cornerstone*, © Hillsong Music

How appropriate that we should sing about the name and use the words 'Jesus' name' because his name is powerful. His name is awesome. His name contains his character. His name contains his ability. His name contains his persona. It's him. He wants us to understand that name and to use that name.

I have three questions for you to close this chapter.

Firstly, have you received him as your Father and been born again?

Secondly, do you respect the names of God? Do you respect his authority? Do you respect his power?

And thirdly, do you pray in the name of Jesus? Do you pray? Because if we pray, we will change things, we will change this world.

Not long ago an article sent to me in an email noted that revival is available. Did you know that? Would you like to see revival in your country? Many would like to see revival in their country. Do you know why we don't see revival in our country? I can tell you quite clearly. There is one reason why we don't see revival in our country. The answer has two parts to it.

One, we don't pray and two, we don't do. That's why we don't have revival in our country. A group of leaders I was speaking to recently concluded that the reason we have no revival is we're not prepared to do the work.

We have too comfortable a life here in this country. Honestly, we've all got a lounge suite, a house, a car, a television. Maybe not everybody has a T.V., but most people have and we like to sit in front of it and do nothing. Do we pray? Because if we pray, (not just pray generally, but pray specifically for a revival in our land) then something will happen as it says in the Lord's Prayer, "your will be done on earth as it is in heaven."

When God interrupts our prayer and says, "So, what are you going to do about it?" we may be motivated to actually start to take some faith and begin to do something towards revival, with the result of God honouring our faith and answering our prayer.

So, what are you going to do about it? If we do something about it, we will see revival. That is my challenge to you today, that we might pray, that we might pray with knowledge, that we might pray with authority and that we might pray with power and then, let us get out and do the things that we pray for. God send us people. "Oh," he says, "you go out and find the people." People won't come into the church generally. Maybe a few people here and there, but there are millions of them out there that will never come in, but we can go out there to them. We can start doing something to reach out to them and it's amazing, when you start telling people about Jesus amazing things happen.

At my work, we're praying for a guy in Nepal who's holding a Christian camp for kids in Nepal. He's doing two camps, one for the leaders and one for youngsters. He's expecting five hundred kids at each. In Nepal, he's doing the work. There's not a lot of Christianity in Nepal but he's doing the work.

Let's pray and think about the challenges that I've set before you in this chapter.

"Heavenly Father, I thank you for your word and I thank you Lord that you have spoken to me. Father, I pray that your word will take root in my heart, that fruit will be reproduced from it. Father, I thank you for your word helping me to grow in you, to receive your word and to act upon it in Jesus' name. Amen.

3

Your Kingdom Come, Your Will be Done

Matthew Chapter 6:9-13 NIV, "This then is how you should pray. Our Father in heaven, hallowed be your name. Your kingdom come, your will be done in earth as it is in heaven. Give us today our daily bread. And forgive us our debts, as we also have forgiven our debtors. And lead us not into temptation, but deliver us from the evil one."

Shall we pray? We just did. Oh, that was not a prayer, that was an instruction about life and prayer, and in the last chapter I said we'd take a walk through this prayer, The Lord's Prayer, as it is known; but let us pray now.

PRAYER
Heavenly Father, we do thank you for your love for us and we thank you for your grace in teaching us how to relate with you.

Father, we thank you for your word and we pray that today, it will be instructional and it will be helpful and it will be inspirational and it will be correctional in our lives in Jesus' name. Amen.

I want to take that little bit that says, "Thy kingdom come, thy will be done on earth as it is in heaven."

Did you ever think about it? You probably prayed it sometime or other, did you ever think about it? Thy will be done on earth as it is in heaven. I want us to think about it.

It's commonly thought to be a prayer of hastening the day of the coming of the Lord. However, I suspect that it's more – because it's not in the form of a request or in the form of a question, but in the form of a statement. It is not asking God "Is He going to come?" It's not praying, "Lord, please come." Rather it is saying "Your kingdom come." It's a statement, a statement of fact. It's a faith statement. It's a statement that is declaring something.

This prayer is in fact, not some little mamby pamby prayer that we've repeated since childhood. Rather, this is a glorious, fantastic, amazing statement of faith with which the people of God can change the world they live in.

"Your kingdom come, your will be done on earth as it is in heaven." It is a statement of fact, a faith statement, "Lord, we are declaring your kingdom that is in heaven, to be here on earth." This is the central message of all Christ's teaching. He teaches about the kingdom.

I get very upset sometimes when people promote the church. Jesus didn't talk about the church much. He only actually mentioned it twice. But he spoke many, many times about the kingdom. He said, "The kingdom of heaven." He says here, "Your kingdom come." The kingdom is what Jesus wants to establish on the earth, His kingdom.

Matthew Henry's commentary suggests that the prayer for the coming of the kingdom is because the kingdom is at hand and that Christ taught that we should pray for it to be fulfilled because its time has come. But I say this, not as a request for that time to come, but as a statement of us declaring that, 'the time has come.'

I actually believe that you and I are the people who have been given the challenge to bring about the return of the Lord Jesus Christ. Men and women have come and gone for two thousand years since Jesus lived on the earth, and He has not yet returned as He promised; but it is possible in our lifetime. In fact, it's possible in the next five years for Jesus to return.

It's not possible for Jesus to return today, tomorrow or next week, (although you should live as though He may), because there are some things that He said must happen that have not yet happened. This kingdom must be preached in the entire world and then the end will come. This kingdom has not yet been preached in the entire world. There are places yet for this kingdom to be preached.

Just imagine with me for a second; what if we, as individuals and as a church, got it into our head that we could actually bring about the return of the Lord Jesus Christ, and we actually did something towards what He said should happen before the end comes. That we went and preached the gospel to all the known world, and then the end would come. This prayer would then be fulfilled because we have helped to bring about the return of the Lord.

It has been physically possible since about the 1980's for us to preach the gospel to the entire world within a five-year period. Now, that is actually a bit of an indictment on the church because we could have done it forty years ago with the technologies and the people that were available even then. But we sat in church and did nothing.

We have radios, we have computers, we have telephones, we have planes, we have transport and technologies to allow us to live in unfriendly and unfamiliar environments. You can get anywhere on this planet within two or three days, even to the most remote places. Just imagine that by this time next week you could be having a revival somewhere in the jungles of Sumatra or in the jungles of Congo. It's possible. You could go tomorrow. You could be there in two days or less, you could have a revival within four days.

This statement, "Thy kingdom come, thy will be done on earth as it is in heaven" is like we are declaring it to be. When we pray, we declare it to be. I'm declaring the kingdom of God just as God, at the beginning of time, declared things and they were. He created the worlds by his word. He spoke, "Let there be light. Let there be plants. Let there be animals. Let there be humans." He said, "Let there be" and there was. He actually declared things.

And he said that he has put the same declarative power in us. Let there be – let that same declarative power be in all of us. He calls things that be not as though they were. Past tense. Did you get that? He calls things that be not as though they were. So, he makes things appear out of nothing by speaking to them. You'll find that in Romans 4:17. It's a faith statement like "Let there be light."

Jesus taught us in other places to pray and to speak as He did. Do you remember when he was walking along the road, and he cursed the fig tree? As He's walking along the road, he cursed the fig tree because it didn't have any fruit on it. It just happened to be the wrong season, but he cursed the fig tree. On the way back, that evening, the disciple said, "Master, look, the tree that you cursed has withered." And Jesus gave them a very important lesson.

And this is what he said in verses Mark 11:22-24 KJV "And Jesus answering saith unto them, Have faith in God. For verily I say unto you, That whosoever shall say unto this mountain, Be thou removed, and be thou cast into the sea; and shall not doubt in his heart, but shall believe that those things which he saith shall come to pass; he shall have whatsoever he saith. Therefore I say unto you, What things soever ye desire, when ye pray, believe that ye receive *them*, and ye shall have them. "

He didn't say, "Go and pray for the mountain." He didn't say, "Go and pray about your problem." He said, "Speak to the mountain and cast it into the sea. Speak to it and it will be done."

This is a form of prayer but it's not asking. It's telling. Are you getting that? It's the prayer that tells; it is not the prayer that asks. So often, as Christians, we have come to the Lord in prayer, asking him for something that he has already told us we should command. He's already told us to command our mountains. He has already told us to command the situations. He has already told us to speak healing to the sick. He has already told us to command the problems. He has already told us to command the kingdom of heaven on earth. He has told us to do that.

And yet we come to him cap in hand, "Lord, please, wouldn't you mind, it would be really nice if you could just..." and he's waiting for us. We should not be commanding God to do something; we should be commanding the things on earth that God has already told us to command. We're just doing what he has told us to do. We're not telling God what to do, or how to do his job. Sometimes we want to tell God how to do his job but that's a different matter, isn't it? We're telling the situation (the mountain) what to do at his command.

It's a prayer of allowance. It's letting the kingdom come. I'm letting it come. I'm letting it come in my life. I'm letting the kingdom of God come into my life. I'm letting it come in my sphere of influence. I'm letting it come in my home. I'm letting it come in my work. I'm letting it come in the people that I meet. I'm letting it come in the way that I think, in the way that I behave. I'm letting it come. It's coming more and more and more as I let it. It's getting better, bigger and stronger in me all the time as I become more like Christ. In mankind's eyes I haven't arrived at perfection yet, but God sees me as perfect. Only He sees me as perfect, because when He looks at me, He sees Jesus, my saviour, redeemer, the one who took my place, the one who gave me His righteousness.

I see myself how God sees me, but then I also see me how I see me. Do you get that? There's a bit of a disparity there so I'm going to 'let' some more. I'm going to do some more letting, letting of the kingdom of God come into my life. I'm going to do some more letting the kingdom of God into my life so that I start to behave and act and live like the kingdom of God is living in me.

Let this gospel message, a message of the kingdom of Salvation in Jesus, be preached in my life. Let this message be preached in my community, my sphere, in my world. Let it be preached wherever I am. Let the bounds of the gospel, the message of salvation be enlarged. That the kingdom of the world be made the kingdom of the Christ, and all men subject to it. That's what I'm letting; living in the character of the kingdom.

Wow, that's a tough one, isn't it? Because we looked at our character and we go, "You know, I'd like to be good, but I know me better than that." So, we have to let the kingdom come in our life.

"Thy kingdom come" What is the kingdom? This passage is addressed to the Father, so we're speaking to the Heavenly Father. 'Our Father,' it says in its first words. It's not any kingdom. It's not the kingdom. It's not a kingdom. It is HIS kingdom. I'm letting His kingdom come in my life. Your kingdom come.

I want you to read a few passages that use this phrase 'kingdom', so we might get a little better understanding of what this kingdom is all about. We are going to look through a few chapters of Matthew and read the verses that relate to the kingdom.

Matthew 3:2 NIV and saying, "Repent for the kingdom of heaven has come near."

Matthew 4:23 NIV "Jesus went through Galilee teaching in their synagogues preaching the good news of the kingdom and healing every disease and sickness among the people."

Matthew 5:3 NIV "Blessed are the poor in spirit for theirs is the kingdom of heaven."

Matthew 5:20 NIV "For I tell you that unless your righteousness surpasses that of the Pharisees and the teachers of the law, you will certainly not enter the kingdom of heaven."

Matthew 6:33 NIV "But seek first the kingdom and his righteousness and all these things will be given to you as well."

Matthew 9:35 NIV "Jesus went through all the towns and villages, teaching in their synagogues, preaching the good news of the kingdom and healing every disease and sickness."

Matthew 10:7 NIV "As you go preach this message, the kingdom of heaven has come near."

Matthew 11:12 NIV94 "From the days of John the Baptist until now, the kingdom of heaven has been forcefully advancing and forceful men lay hold of it."

Matthew 12:28 NIV "But if it is by the Spirit of God that I drive out demons, then the kingdom of God has come upon you."

Matthew 13:11 NIV, "He replied, "Because the knowledge of the secrets of the kingdom of heaven has been given to you, but not to them." That's powerful. We'll touch on that again in a minute.

Matthew 13:24 NIV, Jesus told them another parable: "The kingdom of heaven is like a man who sowed good seed in his field.

There is also a series of parables,

Matthew 13:31 NIV, he told them another parable. "The kingdom of heaven is like a mustard seed which a man took and planted in his field."

Matthew 13:33 NIV, He told them still another parable: "The kingdom of heaven is like yeast that a woman took and mixed into about sixty pounds[a] of flour until it worked all through the dough."

Matthew 13:41 NIV, "The Son of Man will send out his angels and they will weed out of his kingdom everything that causes sin and all who do evil."

Are you starting to get a bit of a picture of this kingdom?
The kingdom of heaven is like: -
Verse 44, a treasure hidden in a field.
Verse 45, a merchant looking for fine pearls.
Verse 47, a net thrown into the lake and caught all kinds of fish.
Verse 52, the owner of a house who brings out of his storeroom, new treasures as well as old.

New treasures as well as old. There is new revelation as well as old. Our understanding of the kingdom is expanding and growing.

Matthew 16:19 NIV "I will give you the keys of the kingdom of heaven. Whatever you bind on earth will be bound in heaven. And whatever you loose on earth will be loosed in heaven."

These are the keys of the kingdom. This is the declarative power that God has invested in us. That we might change the earth. You are here not to take up space. You're here to change things, to bring the kingdom of God to this earth, to the environment in which you live and move.

Jesus was teaching the kingdom related to all aspects of life. The kingdom of heaven is at your house when you're having dinner. The kingdom of heaven is in your car when you're driving down the road. The kingdom of heaven is at the service station when you're filling up with petrol. The kingdom of heaven is at your place when you go to work.

The kingdom of heaven is involved in every part of our life. Therefore the kingdom of heaven should be showing through every part of our life. It's not a separate part of our life, our kingdom life or our church life. And then over here I've got my family life, and over here, I've got my social life, and over here, I've got my work life. Over here, I've got my education life. No, we don't have all those separate compartments in our life. It's our life, its one life and there's the kingdom flowing through it in all of those paths.

The kingdom of heaven; God's kingdom, is about having God living through us in all aspects until every part of our community becomes filled with the life of God. This was Jesus' teaching and it was radical in His day. The reason it was radical in His day was because the Israelites had separated or compartmentalized life. They had separated the laity from the priesthood.

Unfortunately, for the next two thousand years after Christ, the church has continued in that vein and yet God never intended that we had a separate laity and priesthood. He intended that all believers should be priests unto God and have access to the Father. He intended that all believers should be people who would be delivering and bringing about the kingdom of God in their environment.

Jesus' teaching about the kingdom was that it would change our life. It would change every part of our life not just, "I'll go to church on Sundays now." Because if you just go to church on Sunday and maybe Wednesday or some other day and that's your religious thing and God is not involved in the rest of your life, then God has not invaded your life. The kingdom of God has not come to you. You just got a religious thing which is kind of what people have done for thousands of years. They've had this religious part of their life, and Jesus condemned that. That's why the Pharisees and the Sadducees and the teachers of the law didn't like him, because he was upsetting their applecart.

He was saying, "No, it's not about having a religious part of your life and then the rest of your life over here." He said, "The religious part of our life should be where we relate with God and that should flow through every other part of our life."

"Thy will be done on earth as it is in heaven." KJV

What a profound statement. When the kingdom comes, the Lord's will is done. That's why he said, "Your kingdom come" that we should be part of delivering and bringing about the kingdom, because when the kingdom comes and people are living in the kingdom, then the Lord's will is done. The Lord's will, will be done when his kingdom is here.

The kingdom is already established and settled in heaven. It's already good. There's no sin there. There's no rebellion. There was once but Lucifer got kicked out. Everybody else learned their lessons. There's no unrighteousness. There's no sickness. There's no lack. There's no pride. There's no selfishness in heaven because the kingdom is there.

That's the kingdom, and the king is on his throne. He told us to say, "Thy kingdom come on earth;" and we think, "Wouldn't it be wonderful if..." but don't believe that it is actually possible. It is actually possible for us to bring the kingdom of heaven to earth, and this is why Jesus told us and taught us to pray in this manner.

I think that if we prayed the Lord's Prayer and I, along with you, probably have prayed it many times and never given a thought to the words that we spoke; but if we would pray, and think about that line, it would consume us for days. I wouldn't be able to get on to the next line of the prayer because I would be consumed by "Lord, let your will be done here in earth." Wherever I am and wherever I go, let me take a portion of your kingdom and let it be seen by the people where I am. Down at the supermarket, the dress shop, the hardware store, where you do go? Let the kingdom come where you are on a daily basis.

The character of the king reigns in the subjects of heaven. We like to think of ourselves as Christian. Oh, we're Christians. Oh, but we don't think about the character of the king.
Is His character reigning in my life?
Would you have done that last night, if you thought about it?
Would you have said that last week, if you thought about it?
Would you have been in that place, if you thought about that?

Let the character of the king reign in us. Making the declaration he told us to make that his kingdom would come on earth as it is in heaven. We know how it is in heaven, so that's the prayer isn't it? We know how it is in heaven. There's no sickness, no pride, no selfishness, no unrighteousness and that's the prayer that we're praying. Lord, let righteousness reign on the earth around me.

Don't make it so general, that it loses its personal effect, i.e.: 'let righteousness reign in my country.' That's fine, pray that, but get a bit more specific. Ask the Lord to let righteousness reign through you wherever you are, wherever you go, to the people that you meet, that your words might declare his righteousness that your words might show that you are living under the headship of the king of heaven.

We may think, 'It's not in our hands.' Wrong. It's not in God's hands to make it happen, it's in our hands. He doesn't change the world. He gives people an opportunity to change. He is saying, "If you'd like to invite me, I'll come and change you. And if I come and change you then you'll actually have an effect on other people."

One Friday night I was talking to one of the young guys, who were with us for the monthly victory meeting, and I sensed that he wasn't quite as comfortable as some of the others. I said, "Hey, how long have you been a Christian?" He said, "Seven days." I said, "That's exciting. That's great." And a little while later I was talking to a young lady and I said to her, "How long have you been a Christian?" She said, "One day."

I could see something start to turn the light on, the light was going on inside, they started to realize something. You can see that they're changing, but you can see that they're not right there yet, but you can see that something is happening in their lives. I'm excited that God wants to use us to bring the kingdom of God to the earth.

He said, "Go ye into all the world, and preach the gospel." He didn't say, "Pray for somebody else to go into all the world and preach the gospel." So, in praying, we are establishing the kingdom of God on earth because our prayers are not mamby pamby. They're not little wishy-washy things they're powerful prayers of faith. They're prayers of declaration. They're prayers that actually change things. Do you know what is the greatest thing that they change? You.

When you start to pray "Lord, let this happen." Something happens in you. Something happens in you that you become emboldened. You become empowered. You become filled with the Spirit. You become the person who says, "I'm not going to lie down and let the devil and evil walk all over me. I'm not going to let that happen to me." And you know what? Other people know you and they see that. They see you stand up. They might not hear you pray but they see you stand up. They see righteousness in your life, at home, at school, at work, at Uni. They see righteousness in you.

When I was younger I worked in a fruit packing shed, it was a pretty noisy place, machinery noise and forklift trucks going around all over the place, it was really quite noisy and I used to sing, (I was just a fairly new Christian), I used to sing the choruses I was learning at church and I would sing at the top of my lungs.

I used to sing choruses all the time, and whenever anybody came close, they would hear me singing. But they'd have to get within about one metre before they could hear me because of the noise in the packing shed. So, I got a bit of a reputation and they used to call me "Bible". They would call out to me, "Hey Bible, come over here."

You see, if you stand for something, it comes out of you. If you're seen to stand for something, people know who you are. Some years later, I was in the main street of Mildura and one of the guys that I had known in the packing shed saw me in the street. He said, "Hey, Bible!" They didn't know what my real name was. They just knew me as Bible.

I would get my Bible and go and sit outside in the sunshine at lunch break and eat my lunch and have a read of my Bible. I would come inside the shed after lunch and I'd sing the words of the choruses. Something about my life was on display.

He calls for us to be people who stand up on the inside. When we pray this prayer, "let your kingdom come." We're praying, "God, let it come in me. Let it come in me because I am your ambassador. I am here on earth to represent you." He tells us that in 2 Corinthians 5:20 that we are His ambassadors. As an ambassador, I'm here to represent the king. I don't belong to this country. I belong to a different country. I don't belong to this world. I belong to a different kingdom. I'm here as a representative of that kingdom. Everything I do, say, act, think should represent that kingdom. But does it?

This kingdom that we represent calls us to take the authority that the kingdom invests in us, calls us to take that and use it. Jesus said the keys of the kingdom and the understanding of the kingdom has been given to us. Well, you think about that for a second. The keys of the kingdom have been given to you. To you. The keys of the kingdom; and not only the keys, but the understanding of the kingdom also. And we just blaze through life not thinking about what is actually happening around us, yet God says He has given us the understanding of the kingdom.

Read those scriptures again. In Matthew 16:19 NIV "I will give you the keys of the kingdom of heaven; whatever you bind on earth will be bound in heaven, whatever you loose on earth will be loosed in heaven." And Matthew 13:11 NIV "The knowledge of the secrets of the kingdom of heaven has been given to you, but not to them." Jesus' words, "Has been given to you, but not to them." Not to who? Not given to the unbelievers. Not given to those who don't declare the kingdom of God.

The secrets of the kingdom of heaven and the knowledge of the secrets of the kingdom of heaven are given to those who live in the kingdom of God by their choice, by their personal character and not to those who don't. Jesus has given the secrets, but we often don't look for the secrets. We don't allow the secrets of the kingdom to come into our life. We don't think deeply enough.

Life is too busy. Who's busy? Are you too busy? Life is too busy for most of us, we actually need to take some time to stop and think deeply and let the secrets of the kingdom of God be born in us. In his book, 'Too Busy Not to Pray', Bill Hybels says, if you're too busy to pray then you're too busy. You need to take some time out to pray. Take some time out because it's when we pray, and I don't mean just repeating prayers, I mean spending some time and letting the Lord wash over you. It's then that we start to think deeply about the things of God. Then we start to get revelation about the word of God. The word of God starts to reveal things to us, helps us to understand how we should then live.

That's my challenge to you today. How will you then live? I challenge you to lay at the foot of the cross all those things in your life that would not honour God...lay them down, leave them. Let Christ be all in all to you. Let His kingdom come in you. Having a kingdom mindset in every aspect of our life; home, work, school, social and family. Have a kingdom mindset in every part of our life.

That is the challenge. What will you do with the challenge? Will you do something with that challenge today? And say, "Yes God, there are parts of my life that I need You to invade. I'm opening this door to you and allowing you to come into my life." So, when we pray, 'Our Father which art in heaven, hallowed be thy name. Your kingdom come, in me, Your will be done, through me, on the earth.' Then we'll see a change taking place. I think it is definitely possible for us to change our communities.

I think it's possible for our communities to get a reputation as being a great place to live. Not just a good place, a GREAT place to live, because there's so much good stuff happening in them, because there are so many good people filled with faith living in them and declaring the kingdom of God over their communities.

People declaring the kingdom of God over their lives, over their communities and it's happening when you go to a supermarket. It's happening when you go to the petrol station. It's happening when you go to work. It's happening in your home. It's happening in your street.

Here's an idea. I went to a street party a few weeks ago, somebody in our street, (I wish it had been me, but it wasn't,) thought it would be a great idea for the street to get together so we could get to know each other. They put a flier in every mail box, "We're having a street party at the end of the street at the park come on Sunday afternoon."

We went. We met some of the people from our street, not everybody came but I met some of the people from our street that I didn't know. In fact, the people that I do know, which are the ones who live really close to me just directly across the road and next door, none of them came. I got to meet people from the other end of the street that I'd never met. Why did I do that? Just to declare the kingdom in my community.

Let's pray.
Father, we thank you for your blessing upon our lives. We thank you for your word that declares your love for us. Father, we thank you for the inspiration that your word is to us. Father, we come and offer You our lives. Father, there have been parts of our lives that we wouldn't be proud of before you. But Father we offer that to you. We offer that to you today Lord, and we say Father, come, let your kingdom reign in me. Thank you, Lord.

4

Give us Today our Daily Bread

Are you happy? Because we praise God; that makes me happy...does it make you happy praising the Lord?

Happiness is not what we're aiming for, but it is still pretty good to be happy, isn't it? Happiness is not the objective though. If I was sad, I would still praise the Lord, because praising the Lord has nothing to do with our emotional state of happiness or otherwise; however it's much better to be happy and praise the Lord.

Actually, joyful is better still. The joy of the Lord is our strength, happiness is subject to our circumstances. You're happy because things are going well and you're not happy if things are not going well, right?

But we can be joyful when things are not going well, because we can get that joy, that inner well of joy that comes up from within when we know the Lord, regardless of the circumstances.

Let's go back to Matthew chapter 6. We've pulled it apart a little bit so far. Starting to read at verse 8 "Do not be like them for your Father knows what you need before you ask him. This then is how you should pray. 'Our Father in heaven, hallowed be your name.'"

We spoke about the relationship that we have with God as Father. We spoke about 'hallowed,' what that means, the holiness of God, the reverence, the awe and the respect. Hallowed be your name.

He sets his name above everything else. His name is above every other name. We spoke about the power of the name and why His name is hallowed, that is because His name is who He is. His name reflects who He is. "Your kingdom come; your will be done." We spoke about that. We said that it's a declaration. We said that's not a request. It's not an asking. It's not a petition. It's a declaration. We're saying, "your will be done". We are responsible for declaring the Lord's will to be done on earth. We're not asking God to come and do it because he has already said, "You do it."

He said, "Go ye into all the world and preach the gospel." He said, "Go ye and heal the sick." He said, "Go ye." therefore, the job is for us to do. We have to declare it in the creative words that God gave us just as He used in the beginning when He said, "Let there be light and let there be sun and moon and stars and planets and animals."

He said, "Let there be." He created by his words and he called out to declare his will on the earth and we know that his will is not completely done on earth yet, because we still have problems. We have social ills. We have evil and crime happening in the world. We have poverty and we have people dying that ought not to die, because of war, famine and disease; because of things that are actually preventable.

He wants His kingdom to come on the earth and he told us to declare it. "Your kingdom come, your will be done on earth as it is in heaven," because we know His will is done in heaven.

Now we can move on to, "Give us today our daily bread."

We have come through the parts where we respect God, we have learned to hallow his name, we understand the importance and value of His name, we've spent considerable time looking at that and making declarations on the earth and the things that we want to see come to pass that are in accordance with his will.

He has told us to speak them into being. Now we come to the part that's for us. "Give us." First of all, it was 'God do this' or 'God thank you for telling me to do this.' But now it's 'God give me.' "Give us this day our daily bread."

Now, you can have whatever you like. I think when He says bread, even though it is actually a reference back to the days of the children of Israel wandering around in the wilderness when God gave them manna from heaven; sometimes called 'bread'. In fact, it probably wasn't bread because it wasn't made from any cereal crops that we know.

Nonetheless, it's a reference back to the bread of heaven. The manna fell and it was strange. They called it manna because they're stuck in the desert and they have no food and Moses cried out to God and God answered, "I will give you bread from heaven. In the morning it will be on the ground. Just go out and pick it up." When they saw it, they didn't know what it was, so they called it 'manna' meaning 'what is it?'

They picked it up and thought, "This is great," and they gathered heaps. Moses said to them, "Just gather enough for the day." They ignored Moses instruction and gathered heaps and they had plenty left thinking they would have some for tomorrow because this phenomenon has never happened before. They're thinking ... 'You know, we will need some tomorrow as well. Don't just gather enough for today.'

So they disobeyed the word of God and they gathered more than enough for today. And what happened to it? The next day, it had all gone off, it smelt awful, and it had weevils in it.

God said to them, "Just gather enough for the day, because tomorrow I'm going to give you fresh bread." Did you ever pass a bakery when they're baking? Oh, fresh bread. Doesn't that smell good?

He said, "I'm going to give you fresh bread every day from heaven." The bread that they gathered from the day before and kept, had gone off and it stank, so they had to get rid of it. Now they just gather enough for one day. They got the idea. But God said, "On the sixth day, I'm going to change the rules a little bit and on the sixth day just gather enough for two days and on the seventh day, the Sabbath, there will not be any and what you gathered on the sixth day will not go off." Isn't that awesome?

There is a rule that applies for five days and then God changes the rule. One rule for the first five days and on the sixth day He changes the rules so that they don't have to go out and work on the seventh day, their Sabbath of rest. There is no gathering the bread on the Sabbath but there is sufficient supply. Isn't that amazing?

God provides supernaturally. Can you see that? The supplying of manna was a supernatural provision, which went on for forty years. That bread from heaven stopped when they crossed the Jordan and went into the Promised Land and they started to raid the people that lived in the land and took the City of Jericho, etc.

They didn't have the manna provision from then on, but for forty years, it was with them. I wonder what it tasted like. You can try and describe a taste to somebody, but if they've never tasted it, it's hard to describe a taste, isn't it?

What does bread taste like? Well, it tastes like bread I suppose. What do strawberries taste like? They taste like strawberries. If you've never had a strawberry, you don't know what strawberries taste like; it's hard to describe a taste.

God had provided supernaturally for them, but they still had to go and gather it. I find that fascinating. He didn't just make it appear in their pantry, he could have, but he didn't, He dropped it from heaven on the ground. Why didn't he just drop it from heaven in their bowls in the kitchen? He could have just as easily, couldn't He? But they still had to go and gather it. What I find is, we've got supernatural provision. There's the supernatural and there's the natural. They still had to do something.

They still had to go out and work to gather it. We said that the Lord's Prayer is not so much about prayer as it is about life. It's about all the aspects of life here and now. I don't think God is just talking about bread. I don't even think he's just talking about food. I think he's talking about all our daily needs; we have other needs besides food, don't we?

Do you have a phone? You have to pay the phone bill, don't you? You can't pay the phone bill with bread. You need some tradable commodity. Oh, I know... why don't we invent something called money and then we can trade that commodity for other things and services that we need? You and I both have other needs besides food, I believe that what God is saying here, is ask me for your daily needs. The daily needs, not just your bread, not just the food on your table.

God provided for them supernaturally. I believe he will provide for us supernaturally, but he also made them work for it. They actually had to go out with a basket and gather it every day and they had to prepare the food. You know, this food, this manna from heaven, I'm sure they would get sick of just eating raw manna every day. I don't even know exactly what it looked and tasted like. But I'm sure some of those ladies would have been a bit creative with their recipes and tried to find creative ways to make manna soufflé, manna quiche, manna pudding, manna toast.

What else could they have done? I'm sure that they would have made manna stew. A little bit of goat meat in there and they would have done something to create different recipes, they lived on manna for forty years. They would have had to do something, wouldn't they?

I think the message here is; God doesn't want us to go without. Now God is saying, this is what you should pray, 'Ask God to meet your daily needs.' Therefore, I think by inference, we can say that God does not want us to be without our daily needs.

He's telling us to ask Him to meet our daily needs and at another point, he talks about the sparrows, saying, "You are worth more than many sparrows" God knows what you need. Just ask Him and He will give it to you.

There's this element that God gives us what we need, but it's not always in the way we expect. God sometimes wants to test our faith to see that we are actually still in faith, still believing God, still expecting God to do something supernatural in our life. The faith element and the natural elements have to work together as they expected and believed God to give them manna from heaven but then they had to work and go out and gather it and prepare it. There's the natural and there's the supernatural. There's a faith element combined in all that.

We've got to believe that He will provide and that we are required to do something in the process of bringing that supernatural event into fruition in our lives, and do you know what I found? I don't know about you, but I found that sometimes I pray, and I ask God, I've got a need and there's a delay. It's as though he hasn't heard me. "God, I've told you three times about this." "God, I've told you four hundred and twenty-seven times about this."

Sometimes there's a delay and we can get a little frustrated, a little annoyed and perhaps we could even lose faith. Perhaps we could even think that God is not going to provide because I've asked him so many times and it hasn't happened.

Well, did God say to ask Him for your daily bread? Did He? "Give us this day our daily bread." That's asking God, isn't it? He's intending to provide. The important issue that I find here is that regardless of how we're traveling, regardless of what the needs are, regardless of how desperate those needs might be and how much past the due date we are, we have to keep the faith. We've asked God. Don't give up the faith just because it seems that God has not provided and because we've asked for them, but we can't see them.

When we ask God, how long do we believe until we give up believing? We believe God until He comes through. That's the essence of asking God in faith.

If it didn't require faith, then the whole gospel message would be just a – oh, just blab it and grab it. You just say it and it happens, but no, it requires faith. It requires us to express our faith and believe that God will do the things that he has promised to do even if it's not quite in the way or the timing that I'm expecting. He's still going to provide for my needs. So don't lose faith during the waiting.

I want to really emphasise the fact that God does want to provide for those needs. 3 John 1:2 NKJV says, "Beloved, I pray that you may prosper in all things and be in health, just as your soul prospers"

God wants us to prosper. He wants us to be in health and he wants you to be happy. That's a prosperous soul. He wants you to be healed, healthy, happy and terrific with all of your needs met. That's his blessing for you.

In Deuteronomy, there's a whole set of laws that God gave the children of Israel through Moses, He goes on to say that there are blessings and there are curses. If you do this, you will get the blessings. If you don't do that, you will get the curses.

At the end of all of that, he says in Deuteronomy 28:47-48 NIV "Because you did not serve the Lord your God joyfully and gladly in the time of prosperity, therefore in hunger and thirst and nakedness and dire poverty, you will serve your enemies the Lord will send against you. He will put an iron yoke on your neck until he has destroyed you."

That's not very exciting, is it? There aren't too many "amens" and "hallelujahs" on that one, but the start of it is so important. "Because you did not serve the Lord your God joyfully and gladly in the time of prosperity," therefore the bad stuff will happen. We need to serve the Lord our God in the good times.

Do you know what happens? If you look at our society, our society largely ignores God. In western countries we are generally prosperous. We live in a blessed country. We have got everything we need. Of course, we have people at different social levels and economic levels, but we have, everything we need. If you're on a government pension and that's all you have, obviously you don't have a lot in comparison to the rest of our society, but you're still amongst the top five percent of the world's wealthy. Think about that. That puts it into perspective for you. We have got plenty and he says because you did not serve the Lord your God, with your whole heart in the time of prosperity, therefore these things will come upon you.

These things are not so pretty. Our societies as a whole have largely ignored God and have largely gone their own way in a time of prosperity. What happens with an individual you meet when something goes wrong in their life?

They call out to God, don't they? This is when they say, "Can you pray for me?" That's when they say, "I wonder if God can help me." That's when they pray a prayer of desperation. "God, help me." In the times of desperation, in the time of great need, whatever that is.

God is not looking to answer the prayers of those that cry to him in their deep need when they have ignored him in the time of prosperity. However, out of his grace he may. We live in an age of grace so he may, but it's his choosing, not ours. We have no right to call upon him and expect him to do something good for us if we have ignored him in the times of prosperity, if we ignored him in the good times.

Prosperity is conditional upon serving the Lord. Having what we need is conditional upon us serving the Lord with gladness and joyfulness. Being happy and thanking him for the abundance of all things that we have around us, and continuing in that prosperity, is conditional. Obviously, there's more to it than the aspect of just you and me as an individual.

As an individual, we need to apply that truth to our lives, but also, I believe it's important that we apply it as a country, as a nation. Just think about your country. Generally speaking, we have not applied that principle and therefore there will come a time of reckoning for our country unless our country comes back to respecting God, honouring God in the time of prosperity.

We have lived in unprecedented times of prosperity in the last hundred years. Nobody ever, (except for kings, but not the masses, not the population as a whole), have lived in the level of prosperity that we have lived. There is a requirement that we honour God with our lives in this time.

Now how do we get to receive then, the things that we have a need of (we have a need of clothes, a need of transport, a need of housing, need of communication and travel as well as food). We have all those things, don't we? How do we get them?

Jesus says, Ask and it will be given you. Seek and you will find. Matthew 7:7 NIV, "Ask and it will be given to you. Seek and you will find. Knock and the door will be opened unto you."

He says we've actually got to ask. He says to us pray this prayer; "Give us this day our daily bread." The requirement upon us is that we would honour God with our lives and with gladness and joyfulness for the abundance of all things in the time of prosperity with the result that he will continue to pour out His blessings on us and meet our daily needs.

Those daily needs are going to come both supernaturally and naturally. The manna fell from heaven, but the people had to go out and gather it.

This is how I believe the process of prospering works, because, "God gave us this day our daily bread," is a process of prosperity. It's a process, having all our daily needs met.

First of all, there's a promise in giving.

God promises that he will give to us if we give to him. We look at the tithe, the Old Testament talks a lot about the tithe. Of course, a lot of that talk is under the law period, when, after Moses came and delivered the law, they followed that law right through until Jesus came to fulfil the law.

But the tithe that was under the law and that we read a lot about actually started before the law. The law came and embodied a principle that was already in Christ.

Malachi tells us to bring the whole tithe into the storehouse. "When there's food in my house," says the Lord, "then I will pour out for you a blessing that you can't contain."

He says, "Bring the tithe into my house." Where did that tithe come from? It's a tenth of what they've earned. But where did the principle start? The principle started with Abraham, when he went out and fought with the five kings and he took the spoils of war. He then met a man called Melchizedek, a priest, king of Salem, prince of peace and a priest of God having neither the beginning of life nor end of days. I wonder who He was.

There's only one person I know who had neither beginning of life nor end of days. Jesus the Messiah, so Melchizedek is seen as a pre-incarnate manifestation of the Son of God; a Christophany. It says that Abraham offered him a tithe or a tenth of everything that he had taken in the spoils of war. He offered to him a gift; as a gift to God, he gave the first tenth. That's where the concept came from. That's where the principles that were embodied in the law came from.

So the tithe is not really the Mosaic law, because right through the New Testament, we're also encouraged to give liberally, to give to meet the needs of the house of God.

It's not that you must give a tithe. When there is enforcement, we come under law about it; but we are to come under liberality about it. I'm free to give a tithe. I'm liberated to give a tithe. It's not a law but a freedom. It's not an obligation but a release. Actually, it releases my finance if I will give a tenth of the increase that I've got. It releases my finance.

It's the Mosaic law embodying the Abrahamic covenant and then into the New Testament we come with the promise of liberality. In Philippians 4:18 KJV it says, "My God will supply all of your needs according to his riches in glory by Christ Jesus." This promise of supply comes because of what the Philippians had been doing.

He says, "You've been generous and liberal in all of your giving. Therefore, my God will supply all of your needs." Do you get it? Because of their liberality, because of their freedom in giving, Paul says that the promise of God will come to you because you have taken and applied the concept and you've not made a law about it.

Jesus was annoyed with the Pharisees and the scribes, He said, "But woe to you Pharisees! For you tithe mint and rue and all manner of herbs, and pass by justice and the love of God. These you ought to have done, without leaving the others undone." Luke 11:42 NKJV However, you cut it down to the leaf. You've cut it down to the exact amount. There's no freedom in that for you. There's no liberality in that for you and you've missed the weightier matters of the law, love and truth and justice. You've done what you should have done but you've done it to the letter without embodying the liberality, the concept of the spirit of giving. It's the spirit of giving that releases the liberality of God in our lives.

When you give an offering, (this is so that we might understand the principles of how the church runs, how the house of God runs), it costs money to hire or buy and maintain a building. It doesn't just come for nothing.

There's a principle that if we give and we bless the house of God, the house of God can do things and the house of God can be established in a community and set up its name, set up its reputation in a community, that we do something in the community.

I remember on my very first trip to India, we went to this poor church (most of their churches were poor in those days), and the pastor that I travelled with, Pastor Cliff Beard, he's an apostle of faith, he had been there before. It was my first trip, it was also the first team that Cliff had taken.

We went to a small church and the offering plate went around; people mostly threw in small coins. Of course, that was 1979, so money was worth more than it is today, but nonetheless, there's one hundred Paise in one Rupee and there was at that time roughly around 30 to 35 Rupees equal one Australian dollar and mostly people were putting in coins. The biggest coin in those days was a one Rupee coin and then you had a one, a two and a five Rupee note.

You would see a few notes in the offering, one and two and possibly a five. But mostly, it was coins in the offering, because that was what the people had. They didn't have a lot of money, but in the offering one day that we were in church, there was an egg in the offering because this person didn't have any money, but had chickens, and chickens lay eggs.

The giver was giving out of their increase. A lady was giving out of what she had and she put an egg in the offering. We were pretty amazed, amused, bewildered perhaps, "Oh, look at that. There's an egg in the offering." We thought it was rather cute until we realised that this person had put in what they had, it reminded me of the story of the lady that Jesus spoke about. Jesus is watching the treasury and all the people come and put money in out of their wealth and out of their abundance. One woman comes in and puts in two tiny coins and He says, "Truly I tell you," he said, "this poor widow has put in more than all the others." Luke 21:3 NIV

The egg in the offering reminded me of that story. One year later, we were back in India, we were back in the same church and Cliff realised it was the same church. He said, "This is the same church that we were in last year where we saw the egg in the offering." He said quietly to the Lord, "If there's an egg in the offering today, I'm going to bless the person that put it in."

The offering was taken up and the offering was brought forward and put at the front and pastor prays over it. We could see there's an egg in the offering. When Cliff got up to speak, he said, "I don't want to embarrass you. I don't want to cause you a problem, but I want to do something very special for the person who put the egg in the offering." Remember, it's just one egg in the offering.

Very reluctantly, the lady who had put it in, came to the front of the church, she was so embarrassed. When she came to the front and Cliff said, "The Lord has looked upon you and seen that you've been generous out of what you have. You've given liberality out of your lack." He says, "I want to bless you," and he gave her a 100 Rupee note, which is like mind-blowing when they might get 10 to 15 rupees a week for working a normal job.

He gave her 100 rupees, (which to us was like three or four dollars, so not anything huge), but to her it was like more than a month's income and this lady just absolutely broke down and wept that he would give her 100 rupees.

We had another experience on that first trip. We went to a place where they wanted to start a church and so they dug a hole and we got a big, big stone and we planted the stone in the hole, to plant the church. Now you know that doesn't start a church, planting a big rock in a hole in the ground. By faith, we planted a church there in that place. When we were back the second year, we went back to conduct the official opening of the building that was built on that place where we planted the first stone because we'd sown in faith, taking up offerings both in the community and back home. And so, a church building became a reality at that place. I've seen similar stories on other occasions.

I remember one time I had graduated from Bible College. I didn't have a great deal of money, I got a job, and a few months after I started my job, the church that I was attending said, we're going to need to get a bus. We've got so many people we've got to pick people up and the youth group which I was leading wanted to go on trips etc.

It was decided that we were going to buy a bus for the church and we needed to take up a special offering for it. We wanted to buy a Toyota Coaster, a 22-seater or something similar.

I just felt touched in my heart that I should put something in for that offering. Now I had gone through Bible College and had run out of money halfway through. I had taken money thinking that it would last me to the end of the course, but it ran out halfway.

I had got to the stage in Bible College that I didn't have any money at all. I kept squeezing that tube of toothpaste. I kept squeezing it and squeezing it. I'm going to get a bit more out of it because there's no money to go buy another tube of toothpaste. There wasn't enough money to buy a stamp to write a letter to ask my parents or anybody to send me money. That was the position I was in.

Just before I got to that last stage, there was an offering in the church at the Bible College. It was for missions in China. Dr. Paul Kaufman who was running Asian Outreach was there and I put in my very last five dollars. "God, I'm going to bless you with this. This is the last five bucks I've got to my name and I've put it in the offering," and then I went through some period of months squeezing the toothpaste and praying, believing God would supply somehow and to cut a long story short, for my twenty first birthday while I was in college, I was given the money that my grandfather had left me from his estate (he had died seven years earlier), he left it in his will just for me, but I was not to receive it until I was twenty one. I got it about a month before my birthday, when I was on a college break.

My parents said, "This is for you for your twenty first birthday." Seven hundred and twenty dollars I got from my grandfather's estate. It seemed like a million dollars at the time because I had absolutely nothing. That was enough to see me through the rest of Bible College. Back in those days, a single guy could live on the smell of an oily rag and so I learned something in that. That five dollars I had sown, I got something back; I got a return on it. I sowed out of my lack and God blessed me.

Then we come back to the story of the church bus. I'm back at the church after Bible College and they want to take up an offering for the bus. I've been saving up a little bit and I've got a job and I've been working and saved up five hundred dollars. Five hundred dollars was a fair bit for me back then and I've saved it up into my bank account.

I have a job, so I've got a source of income tomorrow as well because I can go to work again tomorrow and earn some more money. I put my five hundred in the offering for the bus. That was all I had, but I had a job. I was working in a fruit packing shed. Then two months later a friend of mine, who I had known before college, (he had moved away to live but he came back to visit) showed me what he was doing for a business.

Through that meeting, I actually was able to start my own first business. He showed me about his business and introduced me to the owner of the Uticolour franchise and that became my trade. I became a Uticolour vinyl welder and I started the business. This friend of mine from a few years earlier came back, he happened to show me his business and then my business was born, I believe because God showed me how to give. Not holding back, trusting Him for everything. God showed me how to give in complete faith. He showed me how to give and give all that I had, trusting Him for the outcomes and for my daily bread.

My giving all went from five dollars, then, less than a year later, to five hundred dollars. Both times, it was all I had, God showed me that if you give in faith, expecting that he will provide, then He comes through and He provides and meets your daily needs.

Secondly, where is the right place to give?

Well, the way to give is obviously in faith; but the 'where to give' is another question. If you look in Haggai 1:5-12 NIV it says, "Now this is what the Lord Almighty says: "Give careful thought to your ways. You have planted much, but harvested little. You eat, but never have enough. You drink, but never have your fill. You put on clothes, but are not warm. You earn wages, only to put them in a purse with holes in it."

This is what the Lord Almighty says: "Give careful thought to your ways. Go up into the mountains and bring down timber and build my house, so that I may take pleasure in it and be honoured," says the Lord." "You expected much, but see, it turned out to be little. What you brought home, I blew away. Why?" declares the Lord Almighty. "Because of my house, which remains a ruin, while each of you is busy with your own house. Therefore, because of you the heavens have withheld their dew and the earth its crops. I called for a drought on the fields and the mountains, on the grain, the new wine, the olive oil and everything else the ground produces, on people and livestock, and on all the labour of your hands."

Why was there a drought? Why was there a shortage? Why did they have money, but it seems to do nothing; because they put it into a bag with holes. They wanted to spend it on their own desires instead of first serving the house of God. Here He is saying that you've not brought down the wood and the timber and you've not built the house of God; therefore, these things, these calamities, (not so much disasters, but the shortages in your life) are because you've not put God first in your life.

We need to bring the first part of our income to the house of God to honour God in our life and finance. The house of God was lying waste and that is why their lives had gone to ruin. So, our giving is not giving to a building per se, although the money we give may or may not go to an actual building (people do need buildings to meet in), but we are building people into a church. We are giving to God to establish His church in a community.

You know that the church is not a building. The church is people and the effect of people in the community, and the reputation that body of people has in the community for doing good. So that's what we're building and that is what our giving to God is used for.

It's about establishing the kingdom of God in the area where you live.

Thirdly, how do we give?
2 Corinthians 9:7 says that we should give cheerfully. Verse 8 says, that having all things, (we have all things) we should give cheerfully. In verse 10 it says that he will give you seed but you must sow, so you're a farmer. You plant the seeds and the seeds produce crops.

You wait for the crop to come and then you harvest the crop. It doesn't matter what kind of crop you put in. You put in a cereal crop that grows up like grass whether it be wheat or oats or barley or some other thing.

Then eventually, it produces a head, or other seeds produce flowers which have seed in them, and those seeds are the seeds for growing more flowers. God says he gives us a seed but he gives us seed to sow, not just seed to eat.

If you eat all the seeds, you have nothing to sow for the next year's harvest. My wife's dad was a wheat farmer, he would get us out there every year in the paddock with the trucks and the combine harvester and we would bring in truckloads of wheat seed. But then he would take some of that wheat seed and he would put it in storage for next year and he would sell the rest.

When it comes time to sow the seed again for next year's crop, he would take the seed that he has put into storage and sow it in the ground. You sow it in the ground and you get another crop. You can't sell all your seeds. We can't eat all our seeds. You've got to save some to sow and that's the principle that he's applying here in Second Corinthians.

In Exodus, Moses took up an incredible offering. He shared with God's people the vision of what God had shown him while he was on the mountain alone with God. He said that God had shown him to build a tabernacle, a tabernacle for the house of God. It was to be a tent because they were nomadic people, they were moving from place to place. They couldn't build a stone structure because they weren't in the Promised Land yet. This tent needed a wooden frame with different animal skins on it as coverings; they needed all these furniture items and things in it and needed all this gold to make it beautiful. Moses went on to ask them to bring an offering for it. Bring an offering of silver and gold and bronze and wood etc. Bring an offering of linen and cloth and bring an offering of skins, bring all this stuff. He implored them to bring the offering so that they could make this amazing tabernacle where God would meet with them.

In other words, he was preparing the building for their worship and the people came, they brought, and they brought. He said, "Keep bringing all this stuff." So, the people got behind the spirit of what it was all about and they were making things and they were bringing things and they were melting down their earrings and bringing gold, until Moses had to say, "Whoa! Whoa! Hold up. We've got more than enough."

Isn't that incredible? How many times have you heard that in church? Stop giving. We've got more than enough. See, that was under the Old Testament. But that was a principle of generous and liberal giving not law-bound giving.

In another Old Testament case Jacob went to work for his Uncle Laban, who had a beautiful daughter called Rachel. Jacob wanted to marry Rachel, but his uncle said, "You can work for me seven years and you can have my daughter." Jacob thought that was a fairly good deal. He was smitten with love and would probably have done anything to get the girl. So, he agreed and of course Laban cheated him by giving him the eldest daughter, Leah. Jacob said to Laban, "That's not the daughter I wanted," Laban replied, "But you've already married her," and he added, "You will have to work for me for another seven years for Rachel," which Jacob did and Laban gave him the daughter he had originally wanted, so Jacob worked for Laban for a total of fourteen years.

Then he continued to work for him and by this stage, he had been married for twenty years and had a bunch of kids, plus God had given him lots of strategies about the flock that he looked after for Laban.

A lot of that flock actually became his, but he still lived in Laban's house and he's still under Laban's rules and so it's not really his. You know what I mean? It's his but it's not his. He has not manifested it. He has not moved out of Laban's control. It's still Laban's flock. But he's kind of responsible for it, but still under Laban's authority.

It wasn't until Jacob moved out of Laban's household, that the flocks actually became his. The flocks that were legally his, became experientially his when he moved out. We need to see that the planting of the seed is the beginning that starts up the process. Jacob believed God would give him things; flocks, etc. so he made a deal with Laban that the spotted and streaked lambs and goats born to Laban's flock would be his and whenever the sheep and goats mated Jacob by faith would hold out the sticks with the stripes on them before the mating animals and most of the flock bore spotted and streaked babies which became his, and so God blessed him that way, in the planting, in the faith stages.

But he waited the best part of twenty years before it actually became his and then he walked away with prosperity. But the prosperity came from the planting; it came out of keeping faith through that time, keeping faith through twenty years of sowing and trusting God.

Keeping a faith confession through the period between when we plant and when we receive is so important. Hopefully not everything you wait for is going to take twenty years! For example, like in praying for today's lunch; hopefully it doesn't take twenty years before you get it, but we need to keep faith going through that period, through that process of believing God, putting the seed out and waiting for the germination, growth and harvest.

First you are planting, believing God and expecting for your harvest to come along. While you are waiting, and it seems as though nothing is happening; don't dig up the seed out of the ground to see if it's growing. Don't say, "Oh, I wonder if that seed is growing. I will dig it up and have a look," because you will wreck the seed. Don't spoil your faith confession by moving away from what you believed because you can't see any evidence of it. It's working. It's germinating under the ground and then it comes to fruition.

But even then, when it grows a little, you don't harvest it because it's not ready and even when the first part of the grain or the ear of the crop appears, you still don't harvest it because most of it is still green and it's no good. You have to wait until it's all dried out and then you harvest it.

We don't take the harvest when it first appears. We actually wait for it to be a God-blessing for the whole harvest to come. So don't pray and then just say, "Well, I will grab this," because it's not ready yet and God has this strange way of just saying, "Just hang loose there just a moment longer and I will bless you really good."

Instead of getting one grain out of that ear, you're going to get one hundred. You just wait a little bit longer until it's all ripe and ready. Listen to the voice of the Holy Spirit. Let him guide you on that and don't pick your crops before they're ready.

For example, one of the ways that I receive is when I just get lost in worship. I want to just close my eyes and worship. I want to remember the words of the song, so I don't have to keep looking at the screen.

I want to raise my hands and I just want to worship God. I don't want to think about other stuff, like the drama we had with the PA system beforehand and what happened during last week and who I've got to talk to on Monday; I don't want to think about any of that. I just want to worship God.

Monday will come and I will think about those things then. I want to worship God now and I want to get lost in his presence. I've seen the reality of that as I worship, that is what brings the release of God in our life.

We pray, "Give us this day our daily bread." I think that the giving from God to us comes in the time of worship and it's not necessarily money falling from the ceiling, but God is going to bless us as we bless him. As we bless him, that's a principle that I've seen time and time again and it's right through the word of God.

If we give to God, God gives to us. We can receive in the worship. I remember one time I was preaching in Victor Harbour, South Australia a long, long time ago and enormous worship was going on. There was a lady sitting halfway down the aisle and suddenly during the singing and worship she started a demonic manifestation, then she gets delivered from demonic power right there in the middle of the worship service.

Nobody came near her. Nobody touched her. Nobody prayed for her. Nobody did anything. Just the presence of God was so real in that worship service because we just got lost in his presence and the power of God came on people.

Another lady got healed in the worship service. Nobody prayed for her. She just got healed in the worship service because we expected God to come, and we worshipped Him.

When we worship, let's concentrate on the worship and think about just Him, the word says He's going to give to us our needs.

How are you receiving?
We have a format of prayer that Jesus has given us. He says pray to God ask Him to give you your daily needs. When He gives them to you, what do you do? Think about this. What if it doesn't come through your expected way? Most of us expect to go out and work a job and get paid and get money for wages and trade that for things that we need, that's probably your expected way of receiving from God for your daily needs, or maybe you've got an investment and the investment pays a return and you use that return to buy your needs.

That's the expected way or common way, but God can actually do things different ways. Sometimes God will provide for you through somebody else, through a person unexpectedly, blessing you with something.

Don't be shy about receiving. I see sometimes people get embarrassed. They don't want to receive something from somebody. Somebody wants to offer them something; wants to give them something and they don't want to accept it.

They can often be heard saying "No, no, no, you don't need to do that." Maybe you've heard that. Maybe you've said it yourself!

What are we actually doing when we do that is denying two things; first, we are denying God's blessing. We pray for him to give us our daily needs and now He's trying to and we're not letting Him!

The second thing we are denying, is a blessing for the person giving. We deny them the blessing that they will get for giving because we wouldn't take the thing that God wants to give to us through them.

So don't be bashful about somebody giving you something, whatever it might be. It doesn't have to be money; it might be a tangible thing. Some years ago Joy and I used to go up to the supermarket after night church and come home with heaps of cheap groceries, we would go in to get some bread and milk at the supermarket and we would go in at about 10pm on a Sunday night as they were closing out all the fresh produce to get rid of it, and we got ridiculously cheap prices.

We would come home with bread buns, vegetables and all kinds of other things for three dollars. We've got arms full of food. God sometimes just blesses you. When somebody wants to give you something, just let those people receive their blessing by graciously receiving their gift because we see that God is answering our prayers. "God give me this day my daily needs" and let God bless them in the process of giving. So don't refuse to receive it because we want our needs met and we want God to be able to bless us, but we also want others to have their needs met and they are planting seeds to get their needs met.

We want to be able to bless other people as well so receive the abundance that comes from being a liberal giver and receive it happily, graciously and liberally. Are you ready to receive now? Are you ready to receive the blessing of God?

It says in 2 Peter 1:3 NKJV "as His divine power has given to us all things that pertain to life and godliness, through the knowledge of Him who called us by glory and virtue," He has given unto us all things that pertain to life and godliness; both natural and supernatural, He gives us the natural and He gives us the spiritual. He has given us all those things and so I'm expecting that the abundance of God will come upon our lives, come upon your life, come upon my life, come upon the church and come upon us, so that in abundance we can be liberal givers also. You can't give what you don't have, so in order to be a generous giving person you need to have something to give. Let the abundance come to you, so you can be liberal and then we can be the kind of generous people that God expects us to be because as His church, we're liberal, because the church has sufficient to meet its needs. It can be liberal in supporting others and blessing others as well.

"Give us this day our daily bread," is not just a give me, give me, give me, demand on God, but let us understand the process and the principles behind prospering, so that we might have enough for ourself and have enough to meet every other need that I come across as well. There are plenty of needs in the world and there always will be, so we will have to be selective in how we choose those needs; but isn't it good to be able to bless somebody else and to say, "I've enough. I've got more than enough. Let's bless somebody else with what we've got?"

We want to be able to do that as the church. Obviously we have to pay our own way, cover our own operating expenses from the giving within the church. So we need to be liberal people. If we're liberal people and the church is blessed, then the church has sufficient to be able to bless others as well and it has been great to be able to bless the speakers that we've had come, but there are other things that we can do as well and we want to explore that as we go, giving into our community and beyond.

Therefore, let us keep these thoughts in mind, let us pray together now. When you pray the Lord's Prayer, "Give us this day our daily bread," you will remember the liberality that came upon the church to give, so that God would meet their needs.

Pray like this

Heavenly Father, for this day, I thank you and for your blessings I thank you and for your promise to meet all my needs according to your riches in glory, I thank you; so God, I thank you that you will help me to be both a prosperous and generous person, because I have learned to live in your principles of prosperity. I ask for you to give me my daily needs and pour out Your blessing upon me that I might bless You, bless the church and bless those around me. Father, so that the church might prosper and bless others in Jesus' name. I thank you for that Father and thank you that you've helped me to be a liberal person in Jesus' name. Amen.

5

Forgive us our Debts

The next part of the Lord's Prayer we are reading is Matthew 6:12. Check this out in your Bible. Make sure you take your Bible along with you to church, if you've got a bible with you, you will be able to follow along with your preacher, it is always good to check what they are saying is actually in the Bible.

Reading from Matthew 6:8-13 NIV just to refresh us, Jesus is speaking and he says, "Do not be like them for your Father knows what you need before you ask him. This then is how you should pray. Our Father in heaven, hallowed be your name. Your kingdom come. Your will be done on earth as it is in heaven. Give us today our daily bread. Forgive us our debts as we also have forgiven our debtors and lead us not into temptation, but deliver us from the evil one."

Picking up now at verse 12, it says, "Forgive us our debts as we have also forgiven our debtors." It sounds a bit like, "God, can I get out of my credit card debt?" which would be pretty nice, but that's actually not what he's talking about. Following you will see a couple of other translations of that verse, so that we can get a more complete understanding. The Message Bible says it like this, "Keep us forgiven with you and forgiving others." MSG. The Contemporary English Version says, "Forgive us for doing wrong as we forgive others." CEV. So it's not about debt as in the money that we owe, but it's about the things that we owe, the things that we have done wrong, the lifestyle that we've chosen incorrectly before God which is why it says, "Forgive us our sins," or in some versions our debts or forgive us for our wrongdoings as we forgive others.

As I started to think about that, I thought, "Well, that's the whole central point of the cross, isn't it?" The whole purpose of Easter is that we remember our sins are forgiven. The whole purpose of the cross is so we can know that we have forgiveness, because Jesus came to give us forgiveness. He taught it here, this is his teaching about prayer and remember we've said that the Lord's Prayer is not so much about prayer, it's about life. It's about the way we should live. It's an instruction for living.

This is an instruction for living as much as it is an instruction about praying. Praying is about living because we should pray about our life. Our life should be a prayer. Jesus' instruction in the Lord's Prayer is about how to live our life. Jesus teaches us that an important aspect of life, and therefore prayer, is forgiveness.

Well, if we will just leave it there, nobody will get convicted. So maybe we should just move on. Oops, I'm sorry. Requesting and giving of forgiveness should be in our prayer. It should be in our life, the requesting of, and the giving of forgiveness.

We come to Christ through the concept of forgiveness, our forgiveness. He has forgiven us. We came to Christ through that very concept, we remember, and we rejoice and we're glad that we've been forgiven because we know regardless of how good or how bad we have been, we know that we had some stuff to be forgiven from. Are we still friends? I hope so, thank you.

We had some stuff to be forgiven from and yet we are reminded that we should need to continue to ask for forgiveness. Why should we ask for forgiveness if we've already been forgiven? This is how you pray. "Forgive us our debts as we have forgiven our debtors." If Jesus is telling us to repeatedly ask for forgiveness and yet the gospel message is about, I've been forgiven, Jesus died once and for all; it's done. He does not have to die on the cross again. I've been forgiven.

Why then do we need to continually ask for forgiveness? Good question. Let me ask you a question. Did you live a perfect, holy, non-compromising life since the time of your conversion? Did you ever make a mistake? Did you ever offend God? Did you ever do something that offended someone?

What about this one? Did you ever do, think or say anything that was not of faith? Did you ever live by your own means? Did you ever live by a worldly example? Did you ever live by your flesh at any point since you asked Christ into your life?

The Bible says that whatsoever is not of faith is sin. So there has been a point in our lives at some stage or other, (may be more or less frequently than others), but at some point, all of us have sinned since we gave our life to Christ, since we've had our sins forgiven and been washed clean.

1 John 1:10 KJV says "If we say that we have not sinned, we make him a liar, and his word is not in us." Therefore, Jesus is telling us that we need to continually be forgiven; I am often asking God for forgiveness. One of the paradoxes of the Christian life is that the more you grow to be like Him, the more you realise that you're not like Him. The more you ask, "God, make me like you," the more you realise that there are parts of you that still need to change.

Well, we've got this ongoing problem of sin. What are we going to do with it? God cannot allow sin to heaven. You know that. In some recent eschatological predictions, some people were expecting the whole world to go up to heaven, but there would be massive confusion in heaven, if heaven is like earth.

However, heaven will not be like earth, God has said that He is holy, His heaven is holy and there is no sin in heaven. We have been forgiven of our past sin, but then we go and do something that offends the holy God, which is sin. Therefore, we need to have that forgiven. Jesus is saying here in this teaching about forgiveness, "Ask for forgiveness, in the same manner as you forgive others." We will come to that in a minute. That sounds like that could be a bit of pressure, but we need to understand this first. In order to be a part of His kingdom, we need that forgiveness.

Forgive us as we forgive them, it says. Here's the question. If we pray the Lord's Prayer and we pray, "Forgive us our debts as we also have forgiven our debtors," past tense. Forgive me as I have forgiven him for the horrible things he said about me this morning.

Have I forgiven him or am I saying, I didn't really mean that, I'll get him back? The Lord's prayer is what Jesus instructed us to pray;

"Please forgive me because I know that I have offended you just as others have offended me." To pray the prayer, I am saying that I have already forgiven others for their offences towards me. The prayer is actually putting the emphasis back on me to be a forgiver, not on God. Can you see that?

This prayer is putting the emphasis on me that I should forgive others, so that God might forgive me. It's not, "God, You forgive me and then I will be able to forgive them." It's the other way around. It's, "God, I have forgiven him. Now will you forgive me?" We don't think of it that way often, do we? We think of it as God owes us forgiveness because He's God and He's majestic and He's merciful and he owes us forgiveness. No, he doesn't. He doesn't owe us forgiveness. He has actually made it conditional. Forgiveness is not automatic. Forgiveness comes to us when we extend forgiveness to others.

It's much easier to request it than to give it, wouldn't you agree? "God, I need your forgiveness, please. I did it again." Well, He says, "Yes; but that other person, what are you going to do about him or her, the one that really upset you and you just got really angry about it? What are you going to do about that person? Are you going to forgive them?"

Jesus put it like this in Matthew 5 in the sermon on the mountain, which is just a little earlier in that same teaching about the Lord's Prayer. Matthew 5:10 NIV says, "Blessed are those who are persecuted because of righteousness, for theirs is the kingdom of heaven."

Would you like to get persecuted? Blessed are the persecuted for theirs is the kingdom of heaven. Blessed are you when people insult you. Who likes that? Who wants to get insulted? When people insult you, persecute you, and falsely say all kinds of evil against you, it's because of me. Blessed are you. Blessed! Why are you blessed because of that? I don't see anybody putting their hands up, really wanting that stuff.

I read the book by the Chinese Brother Yun, Heavenly Man. Did you read that book? The things he went through, you wouldn't dream of it; you wouldn't imagine it in your wildest dreams, the persecution, the terror, the torment, the pain, the affliction and deprivation of basic human rights.

To think that you could actually live in a place and actually have a meal every day and not be beaten every single day, which would be nice, wouldn't it? To not be beaten every single day, but Brother Yun was beaten, and he had no grudge. He had no animosity. He had no hatred towards his captors and every prison they put him in, he would win the prisoners and some of the guards to the Lord. They kept moving him because he was changing the culture in the prison; he thought it was good because he would just win more people to the Lord in another prison.

Peter asked Jesus this question, "How many times should I forgive?" Matthew 18:21 NIV says, "Then Peter came to Jesus and asked, 'Lord, how many times shall I forgive my brother when he sins against me? Up to seven times?" Meaning, as many as seven times perhaps? I'm feeling really good. I've been with you a long time Jesus and I've learned a lot. Maybe it's as much as seven times I should forgive my brother who offends me, that's a lot, which must be pretty holy!

Jesus answered, verse 22 "I tell you not seven times but seventy-seven times." Now that's the NIV. If you look it up in the King James Version, it says, "But until seventy times seven." Seventy times seven is four hundred and ninety. But who's counting? The point was not the count. The point was the concept. Jesus was not saying keep a record and when you get up to that number, stop. He was saying the concept of forgiveness goes on and on and on and on and on. He wasn't talking about counting.

You see, we sometimes remember what people do to us. We remember that they're not faithful towards us, that they're not loyal to us. They speak behind our back about us wrongly and we judge them accordingly. The Bible tells us that forgiveness for us comes from the forgiveness that we give out.

There's a story in Matthew 18:23-24 NIV94. "Therefore the kingdom of heaven is like a king who wanted to settle accounts with his servants. As he began the settlement, a man who owed him 10,000 talents was brought to him." Now we understand 10,000 talents was a very large amount of money.

Let's say – I don't know if this exactly equates. Let's say you owe somebody a million US dollars. It's such a large sum of money that if you're earning $50,000 a year, you're just never going to be able to pay that back. That's the concept of the predicament this guy is in. It's beyond the possibility of him paying back 10,000 talents. The king began the settlement and the man who owed him 10,000 talents was brought to him.

"Since he was not able to pay, the master ordered that he and his wife and his children and all that he had be sold to repay the debt.

The servant fell on his knees before him. 'Be patient with me,' he begged, 'and I will pay back everything.' The servant's master took pity on him, cancelled the debt and let him go."

Did you know that? He cancelled the debt. He didn't just say, "I will give you time." He didn't say, "Let's work out an arrangement," which your bank is likely to say if you get into trouble with them. He cancelled the debt and let him go just because the guy asked for forgiveness.

"However when the servant went out, he went and found one of his fellow servants who owed him 100 dinari, (twenty dollars). He grabbed him and began to choke him. 'Pay back what you owe me!' he demanded. His fellow servant fell to his knees and begged him, 'Be patient with me and I will pay you back,' but he refused. Instead, he went off and had the man thrown into prison until he could pay the debt."

"When the other servants saw what had happened, they were greatly distressed and went and told their master everything that happened. Then the master called that servant in. 'You wicked servant!' he said, 'I cancelled all that debt of yours because you begged me to. Shouldn't you have had mercy on your fellow servant just as I had on you?' In anger, his master turned him over to the jailers to be tortured until he should pay back what he owed. This is how my heavenly Father will treat you, each of you, unless you forgive your brother from your heart."

They are pretty strong words, aren't they? This is how my heavenly Father will treat you unless you forgive. Divine mercy is really the only basis that we can use for human forgiveness. Just as my

Father forgave me in the beginning when I first came to him with a debt that was insurmountable and unpayable, so I must cancel the debt of another toward me.

He said, "Now, I've given you an example. You have been freed from your debt." We go on committing offences against our holy God and he tells us to come and ask for forgiveness continually for those things. But he says use the divine example as your example for living because we can't put forgiveness into place in our lives unless we use an example, unless we use the example that God gave to us.

Doesn't it help us to get a different take on asking God for forgiveness when we look at stories like that? It's no longer, "God, you owe it to me because you're a merciful God and I need it," but now it's more like, "God, because I need your forgiveness, help me to be generous in my forgiving." We need to really get this, because I need forgiveness, God help me to be generous in my forgiving.

Jesus not only taught about forgiveness, but he was also the perfect example of forgiveness. Jesus lived up to the things that he taught. Mostly we would like to live up to the things we teach and sometimes we do; but we're human and occasionally we do not and that's when the world points the finger and says, "Hypocrites! You say one thing and do another." Well, OK, guilty. Lord, I need your forgiveness. Now recognising that I need this forgiveness, I need to practise forgiveness. I need to practise the thing that I need to receive.

This is what Jesus was going through when they crucified him and he said on the cross, "Father, forgive them. They know not what they do."

As we get a sliver of understanding of what Jesus was going through when He said, "Father forgive them, they don't know what they are doing," let us take a look at what crucifixion is.

Crucifixion

A medical doctor provides a physical description.

The cross is placed on the ground and the exhausted man is quickly thrown backwards with his shoulders against the wood. The legionnaire feels for the depression at the front of the wrist. He drives a heavy, square wrought-iron nail through the wrist and deep into the wood.

Do you feel that?

Quickly he moves to the other side and repeats the action, being careful not to pull the arms too tightly, but to allow some flex and movement. The cross is then lifted into place.

The left foot is pressed backward against the right foot, and with both feet extended, toes down, a nail is driven through the arch of each, leaving the knees flexed. The victim is now crucified.

As he slowly sags down with more weight on the nails in the wrists, excruciating, fiery pain shoots along the fingers and up the arms to explode in the brain. The nails in the wrists are putting pressure on the median nerves. As he pushes himself upward to avoid this stretching torment, he places the full weight on the nail through his feet. Again, he feels the searing agony of the nail tearing through the nerves between the bones of the feet.

As the arms fatigue, cramps sweep through the muscles, knotting them in deep, relentless, throbbing pain. With these cramps comes the inability to push himself upward to breathe. Air can be drawn into the lungs but not exhaled. He fights to raise himself in order to get even one small breath. Finally, carbon dioxide builds up in the lungs and in the blood stream, and the cramps partially subside. Spasmodically he is able to push himself upward to exhale and bring in life-giving oxygen.

Hours of this limitless pain, cycles of twisting, joint-rending cramps, intermittent partial asphyxiation, searing pain as tissue is torn from his lacerated back as he moves up and down against the rough timber. Then another agony begins: a deep, crushing pain deep in the chest as the pericardium slowly fills with serum and begins to compress the heart.

It is now almost over. The loss of tissue fluids has reached a critical level. The compressed heart is struggling to pump thick, heavy, sluggish blood into the tissues. The tortured lungs are making a frantic effort to gasp in small gulps of air. He can feel the chill of death creeping through his tissues. Finally, he can allow his body to die.

All this the bible records with the simple words, "And they crucified him."

What wondrous love is this? The pain, the agony, the torment, which was only the crucifixion. There was also the torture beforehand, and he said, "Father, forgive them. They know not what they're doing."

We feel like we want to get somebody back that said something nasty to us. Jesus died on the cross, and after the crucifixion, (I'm just using a little bit of my sanctified imagination - I'm not sure how sanctified it is). But nonetheless, there was a party going on. There was a yahooing and the celebration and a feast in hell as the devil and his angels congratulated themselves on killing the son of God. What a party! We won! We won!

Then there came a sound, thud, thud, thud, thud, and the sound got louder and louder as the triumphant and the victorious Christ marched into hell. The scripture records it like this. In Ephesians 4:8-10 NKJV it says, "he led captivity captive." He marched into hell and took captive those who had been held by Satan up until that time.

In Colossians 2:15, it tells us that he has disarmed the powers of darkness and made a show of them openly; triumphant over them because of the cross. The gospels tell us nothing about what happened between this crucifixion and the resurrection, except that the disciples were distraught. However, John's book of The Revelation of Jesus Christ, tells us what happened. In chapter 1:17b-18 KJV Jesus says, "Fear not; I am the first and the last: I am he that liveth, and was dead; and behold, I am alive for evermore, Amen; and have the keys of hell and of death."

WHERE DID HE GET THOSE KEYS FROM? He went and took them from Satan who had them. There was a great fear and trembling came over that party down there as the sound of the Son of God approached, because they thought they had won. They thought they crucified the Lord of glory. They thought, that's it, He is finished. He's done; but that was the purpose He came for. He came and he took the keys of hell and of death.

We're searching for healing. We're searching for forgiveness. We're searching for peace in our lives. Maybe we need to let some of Jesus' teachings flow through us and look for opportunities to forgive others.

If you stay in a church long enough or a job or a family or any group of people for that matter, the church is not any different, you're going to get the opportunity to forgive, because somebody is going to say or do something at which you could easily be offended. It happens in families. It happens at work. It happens in school and university. It happens in any kind of group of people. It happens in church. So how strong are you going to be? Are you going to be a Christian or are you going to be one who is offended and says, "I'm going. I'm out of here"? Because I've seen it so often; people get offended in church.

This is a place where we should learn about forgiveness. This is a place where we should learn, if forgiveness was easy, the world would do it, but they don't do it because it's actually difficult. It's actually difficult to forgive someone who has offended you or hurt you or pained you or done something malicious towards you. It's actually quite difficult.

However, the more you do it, the easier it gets and the more we remember that Jesus did it for us, the more we're inclined to do it for someone else, especially when we read the Lord's Prayer where it says, "Forgive me my debts as I have already (past tense) forgiven those who have done things against me."

Well, I'm actually not perfect either. I know I need God to forgive me just as much as you do, in order to do that, I need to forgive others. Sometimes you may even offend people on purpose, but you will offend someone at some point, even unknowingly and others may offend you as well, the purpose of the crucifixion, the purpose of the risen Christ, is that we might know how to actually let go of the things that other people have said and done to us, and that we've hung on to so deeply in our heart.

Today is the day to let it go. Today is the day to be released from that. Jesus was crucified, he has risen again, so we can say, "Well God, I want some of your peace. I want some of your glory. I want some of your forgiveness and I see your word tells me that I've actually got to practise what I want to receive."

Did someone upset you? Did someone make fun of you? Did someone speak a lie about you without cause? Did somebody not respect you? Did someone trash your things? Did someone prefer someone else over you? You thought you were more deserving. Here are some opportunities to practise forgiveness.

To practise our forgiveness, we need to examine our own hearts. When we take the communion, the Bible tells us that we should examine our hearts. Examine ourselves to see if we're worthy to take communion. Are we worthy?

Now forgiveness is not something that takes a long time. The restitution may take time and that's important to do because it shows in practise what has happened in our heart. You may have to do something practically to demonstrate your forgiveness, but forgiveness can happen in a moment. You can actually do all of your forgiveness in the next thirty seconds, and you can live a life of forgiveness because you've decided, "God, I'm not going to hold a grudge. I'm not going to want revenge. I'm not going to look for a way to get that person back for what they've done. I'm just going to move on. I'm going to let that go, water under the bridge, and it's gone and forgotten what they did to me."

As we do that, we can embrace the forgiveness that Jesus offers to us because none of us is perfect. Maybe you would like to have your own communion service with the Lord right now. If you want to get a little piece of bread and some juice and have your own special time of communion and forgiveness, go and prepare that now.

I ask you to examine your own heart. I want you to give it a minute or two of silence to reflect and think about the things that you're going to forgive others for and name them before the Lord, say,

Pray
Lord I forgive _____Name_____ for doing /saying _____Thing they offended you in_____.
Help me not to hold it against them anymore. I forgive them as you forgave me, I receive your love and forgiveness and healing in my life.

"...that the Lord Jesus on the same night in which He was betrayed took bread; and when he had given thanks, he broke it and said, "Take, eat; this is My body which is broken for you; do this in remembrance of me." In the same manner he also took the cup after supper, saying, "This cup is the new covenant in My blood. This do, as often as you drink it, in remembrance of me." 1 Corinthians 11:23-25 NKJV

PRAYER

Lord, we have your example of forgiveness and Father we want to follow your example. Father help me even now to forgive, to wash away the grudges and the hurts and the feelings of vengeance so that I might have a clean slate before you as I come, asking for your forgiveness for my indiscretions.

Eat and drink and thank him for what he has done.

I pray that the love of God is resurrected, reborn, renewed inside your heart. Amen.

6

Lead us not into Temptation but Deliver us from Evil

Now we are coming towards the end of the Lord's Prayer.

It's getting exciting. We've learned a lot about life, but the Lord's Prayer is all about life, isn't it? It's not just about prayer. It's about learning to pray through life and so we come to Matthew 6:13 KJV "And lead us not into temptation, but deliver us from evil," or "from the evil one" depending on the translation.

Let's pray.
Father, we thank you for this revelation. We thank you for the word that you have given us and Father, I pray that each reader would have a revelation in their heart today of your words, something that will quicken them, something that will help them, challenge them, inspire them, speak to this reader's heart Father,

and we thank you that they're covered by the blood of Jesus Christ, and we are forgiven and cleansed and set free.

Lord, they are a new person, a new creation filled with the righteousness of God, I thank you Father that the words that you've set in your Bible, are there to encourage, to strengthen and to lead us on into an overcoming, victorious walk in you.

Father, I thank you that you will help them to live that walk, and reveal it to them through your word today in Jesus' name. Amen.

I'm a little confused by some of the words Jesus spoke at the last supper. He said, "Simon, Simon, Satan has asked to sift all of you as wheat. But I prayed for you, Simon, that your faith may not fail. And when you have turned back, strengthen your brothers." Luke 22:31/32 NIV

Jesus was revealing to Simon, that Satan in the spirit realm had asked God for permission to tempt them, to sift them like wheat, it means to tempt them. I have a question for you - can Satan talk to God? Certainly, it says right here that he did. Satan has asked that he might tempt you or sift you. Wasn't Satan chased out of God's presence, out of the glory? Isn't God's presence too powerful for Satan?

Can God allow Satan to tempt people? Interesting question. Hopefully we will have some answers here. If Satan can talk to God, what does he say? What does he ask? What does he tell? Interesting thought. What do you think? If you were Satan, what would you say to God? (You've probably seen too many movies already, so just put yourself in the actor's role.) You're Satan and your job is to destroy the Christians, stop them from being effective, stop the non-Christians from becoming Christians, so that you can take all the people with you, because you don't want them to go to heaven because God is not going to let you go there.

What is your primary objective? Get your creative thinking going. Your primary objective is to stop them from being effective, isn't it? Stop Christians from being effective. I wonder how you do that. How would you do that if you were Satan? This is a big mind shift for you, I know, but how would you do that? How would you stop Christians from being effective, in sharing their faith, in bringing others to Christ, in praying for the sick, in living a life of victory over their personal circumstances? How would you do that?

How can Satan, (a fallen angel), ask for a child of God? Aren't we too precious in God's eyes for God to give us to Satan? Well, let's have a look at the truth about the methods that Satan uses to keep Christians in bondage, temptation and sin.

Luke 22:31-32 NIV "Simon, Simon, Satan has asked to sift all of you as wheat. But I prayed for you, Simon, that your faith may not fail. And when you have turned back, strengthen your brothers."

Here it says that Jesus saw Satan asking God for permission, to sift the disciples. He was asking God for permission to sift the disciples. Another example of Satan speaking to God is in Job chapter 1. You know the story of Job - the man who had everything and lost it all.

Job 1:6 NIV One day the angels came to present themselves before the Lord, and Satan also came with them. The Lord said to Satan, "Where have you come from?" Satan answered the Lord, "From roaming throughout the earth, going back and forth on it."

Then the Lord said to Satan, "Have you considered my servant Job? There is no one on earth like him; he is blameless and upright, a man who fears God and shuns evil."

It's an interesting reply we get from Satan. "Does Job fear God for nothing?" Satan replied. "Have you not put a hedge around him and his household and everything he has? You have blessed the work of his hands so that his flocks and his herds are spread throughout the land, but stretch out your hand and strike everything he has and he will surely curse you to your face." Job 1:9-11 NIV

That conversation goes on a bit further. I think you know the story. There we see God and Satan having a dialogue, having a conversation about, first of all, what Satan does and then, God pointing out to him one of his upright followers Job and Satan responds with this accusation.

It doesn't actually sound like an accusation at first. It's a statement of fact. He praises and worships you because you bless him, because he has got everything, because he's rich. That's why he worships you. Although that was a statement of fact, it wasn't the whole truth because Satan is assuming that that's the only reason that Job worships God.

However, God is saying no, he's an upright man, he worships and loves me. Satan is making the accusation and saying, "Yes. But he won't love you if you take away all his stuff."

We find this conversation going on and often I think people have overlooked the fact that Satan dialogues with God. Christians have not made a point of understanding the fact that Satan and God are in dialogue. They're actually talking.

We think that God has kicked him out and got nothing further to do with him and one day he's going to get his eternal punishment. But actually, in a couple of places we read already where they actually have a discussion and God didn't rebuke him, God didn't chase him away. God didn't say, "You're not allowed in here."

He listened and conversed with Satan. You know what the name "Satan" means? You know every name has a meaning, don't you? What does the name "Satan" mean? It means "accuser". That's his job. He lives up to his name. He's an accuser. When Satan came into this throne room and he had the conversation with God about Job, he was bringing forth an accusation. He was saying, "God, Job doesn't really love you. He just loves you because you blessed him. He has got all this good stuff. He has got all the animals and he's rich and got servants and everything is going well for him."

But Satan's job is to accuse. Satan had gone into God's presence to accuse Job before God. This is what Satan has told God; Job is not fearing you for nothing. It's because you've put a hedge around him and his household and everything he has. That's why he loves you. That's why he's serving you. It might sound like a statement of fact, but it is actually an accusation.

That's the job of Satan, to accuse. Another way of putting this charge is like this. Job doesn't love you from the bottom of his heart. He fears and loves you because of the richness and the protection that you have given him.

The question is, "Does Job love God from the bottom of his heart?" Satan, up to now, accuses the Christians before God. He does that day and night.

Now he's not continuously in God's presence because the Bible says that he goes to and fro on the earth, seeing what he can do. Paul tells us that he's looking for who he may devour like a roaring lion, he is not a roaring lion but like a roaring lion. He's like a roaring lion seeking someone he may devour. He's looking for someone that he can bring an accusation to God against, accusations about all kinds of things.

In Revelation 12:10 NIV it says, "Then I heard a loud voice in heaven say, 'Now has come, the salvation and the power and the kingdom of our God and the authority of his Messiah, for the accuser of our brothers who accuses them before God day and night has been hurled down.'"

All Christians should take that very, very seriously. Remember at the beginning of the book of Revelation, John says this is the revelation of Jesus Christ, the things which are yet to come, yet to appear. It is the future from the time that John wrote it, and he sees halfway through this revelation, the time when the accuser is cast down. Until that time, he has access to the throne of God.

The Holy Spirit wants us to know that Satan will continue to accuse Christians before God until that day. Until that day, he will be accusing them before God. Satan will never fail to find an accusation against you. Now the main accusation Satan makes before God against us is that we don't love God from the bottom of our hearts. That's his main point he's trying to prove.

With every accusation he brings, he's trying to prove that we don't love God from the bottom of our hearts. Remember the story with Job? He says, "Take all that stuff that you've given him, that hedge of protection you've put around him, take all that away and he will curse you; he won't love you then."

God believes that we have the ability to love him out of our own free will, but Satan is saying, "People only love you because of the goodness that you give to them." And Satan's accusations are not always false. Sometimes he can rightly accuse us. Sometimes.

We know that we don't live a perfect life because at times, there are things that he can accuse us of and we are legitimately guilty of that accusation. Sometimes he comes and he makes accusations supposing that you do something or if this changes for that person, then they won't love you. However, the purpose of Satan's accusations is to get us to fail in the temptation, to fail in the temptation so that he can laugh at God and say, "They don't love you. See? The protection, the things that you've given them, if they are taken away, they won't love you."

Sometimes people accuse us and maybe you've had people accuse you. In our daily lives, accusations can happen. The Pharisees were always looking for accusations against Jesus. They prayed that he would make a mistake. They waited for him to heal on the Sabbath, so that they could accuse him.

They accused him of eating with sinners. They waited for his remarks about paying taxes, so they could find something to accuse him about. They have prepared accusations against him in the case of the woman caught in the act of adultery. They were looking for him to say something contrary to the law or contrary to His own teaching so they could accuse Him of breaking the law or not being consistent with His own teaching. Satan is always looking for something. He's always looking for something to accuse us of and sometimes he might find something, but he's always looking. Sometimes it might be a false accusation. Sometimes it might be a true one. Sometimes, if he cannot find one, he creates an accusation by suggesting false motives. He takes a pound of truth and mixes an ounce of lie with it. It might still look like truth, but it's tainted.

Satan and his army of rebellious angels work outside of heaven, but Satan is using these fallen angels as demons to transverse the earth and find things to accuse people of when he goes back into the presence of God. This is something we need to know. Truth is really important.

Satan still has access to God's presence because his time of destruction has not yet come. When his time of destruction comes, he will no longer have access. But for now, he has that access. The time is coming, as we read in Revelations 12, when he will be cast down.

Another thing that we need to understand is that no one, good, bad, holy or evil, can hide from God. It doesn't matter how good or bad you are. God says that he will find you no matter where you are. He says he has a plan for us. He knows us. Jeremiah tells us he has a plan for you, Jeremiah 29:11 and from before you were born and from before you were formed in your mother's womb. Jeremiah 1:5

He says, "Can any hide himself in secret places so that I shall not see him? says Yahweh. Don't I fill heaven and earth? says Yahweh."

Jeremiah 23:24 WEB You can get on a spaceship and go way out, but God is there in the heavens. You can go and hide in the depths of the sea, but God fills all the earth, He's there.

We can't hide from God. He has a plan for us though and it's a good plan and he wants that good plan to come to pass, but God doesn't make it happen. God prepares things and then allows us to let it happen. In Psalms 139:15b-16 NIV he says, "… when I was woven together in the depths of the earth, your eyes saw my unformed body. All the days ordained for me were written in your book before one of them came to be." You and me both. He knew everything about us, every day of our lives, the good, the bad, the ugly; all our days are written in his book even before we were born.

Did you know that Jesus told us not to worry? He told us, "Don't be anxious for anything. Don't let your heart be troubled." A lady I once knew got that scripture as a word from God. "Let not your heart be troubled and neither let it be afraid." She read that scripture and she said, "Heart, don't be troubled." She had just been told by the doctor that she was in severe danger of a heart attack as she had a major heart problem. She was in her sixties, and she had been teaching five classes of scripture at school and now she had to give it up, so she talked me into doing it for her. I was just twenty years old at the time.

She took that word personally and literally, the one that says, "Let not your heart be troubled." She said, "I won't let my heart be troubled." I only did the scripture classes for her for one term because she came back to school. She came back healed. She has since passed away, but she lived into her nineties and did scripture teaching for almost another twenty years. She just took that word, she said that word, she applied that word, believed it, lived it and it lived in her.

Actually, Jesus wasn't talking about that physical organ (heart) in your body. You know that don't you? When he said, "Let not your heart be troubled," he meant "Don't worry." That's my point.

Jesus has a good plan for us... don't worry. He keeps on reading our file in heaven and looking at all the good stuff that he has prepared for us. I don't think your file in heaven is a manila folder exactly, but it has your name written on the front and it has a page for every day of your life in there and all the good that has happened.

It's already known in heaven, but not known on earth yet and he's looking at all the good stuff and all the things that you're going to do and all the people you're going to influence and all the good things that are going to happen through you. Yet as sceptics we tend to want to say, "Yeah, but what about all the bad stuff I've done as well? The wrong things that I did, I don't really want them in the file."

That's what the cross is for. We come to the cross and we ask for forgiveness and you know what forgiveness means. It's forgive and forget, isn't it? When it's forgiven, it's forgotten. God erases the things that we ask him to forgive, they are not in the file anymore. That page is ripped out, thrown away and totally destroyed. When we ask him, it says, "You will again have compassion on us; you will tread our sins underfoot and hurl all our iniquities into the depths of the sea." Micah 7:19 NIV It also says that he has taken our sins as far as the east is from the west. Psalm 103:12 Now if the earth was flat, that would be a measurable distance but it's a sphere, you can just keep on going east, forever and forever, can't you? You can just keep on going east all the time.

In the same way, God has a plan for us. God has a plan for faith. When Satan reminds us about our past, we need to remind him about his future. God has a plan for him, which we can read about in Revelation 20:10 NIV "And the devil who deceived them was thrown into the lake of burning sulphur where the beast and the false prophet had been thrown. They will be tormented day and night forever and ever." That's God's plan for him. It has already been determined, but the time is not yet.

Satan wants to remind us about our failings, the things that we've done in the past that weren't up to standard, up to God's standard, so he comes along with these accusations of, "Oh, you're not good enough. How can you go and pray? Look at what you just said, did, thought."

We've all been there and we've all met people who are fearful of going to church. They won't go to church because they feel like a hypocrite. They won't go to church because they're not good enough to go to church. They're not good enough to pray even. Have you met those people? They feel they're not good enough to pray. "Oh, I couldn't pray but God wouldn't hear me because of all this stuff that I've done in the past" but we've all done it. They're no different to us church-going Christians.

However, God says, "Come to me all you that labour and are heavily laden and I will give you rest." Matthew 11:28 KJV Another way of putting it would be, "Unburden yourself on me and I will take that off you. I will forgive your sins and heal you from all unrighteousness and I will give you, my righteousness." What an awesome God.

In his mercy, God has planned to forgive us, to provide for us a home in heaven with Him; a provision only obtained through forgiveness, but in God's grace and mercy, he also gave Satan time, but his time has expired and he's not repentant and therefore his judgment has been sealed.

God has always given people time. He gave Satan time, but that time has gone. God's power is above every other power in the heavens and earth. We can see it in just four words he uttered; "Let there be light." Four words and he made light. Pretty awesome God.

He mightily rescued the children of Israel from Egypt. We saw the plagues on the Egyptians. We saw the miracles in the desert. Do you think that if God can do those things, he can rescue you from your situation? Do you think that if he can do that, the difficulties that you find yourself in, whether they be emotional, financial, or physical health, or mental; whether they be relationships, work problems, or whatever they might be, do you think God is big enough to handle them?

We need to bring them to him. The problem is we think we can't bring them to him because we think, "I'm not good enough to bring that to God," but God doesn't care about how good enough we are. It only matters how good enough He is to help us deal with that.

The main reason why God listens to Satan's accusations is that God wants to prove to Satan that we will prove we love God by our actions. That we love God from the bottom of our heart regardless of temptations, regardless of the sifting, regardless of the destruction our enemy Satan, brings upon our lives.

He can't bring destruction upon our lives unless he has permission. You know that. We can give him permission, but God can also give him permission. Do you want to let God give Satan permission to destroy things in your life? If you don't want to let God, give Satan permission then read very carefully from here on.

God may let Satan tempt Christians. Satan will prove to himself that we sincerely love the Father and the Son and the Holy Spirit from the bottom of our hearts by our actions in that time of testing. That's how we will prove that we love God; by not wavering from our faith in Him in the difficulties of testing times.

When Satan gets permission to tempt you, God is not looking for your defeat or failure. God is looking to see you glorify him in that circumstance no matter how difficult it might be.

When Satan succeeds in tempting us, he rejoices and tells God he was right. He has a bit of a laugh at God, but if we succeed in overcoming the temptations, then Satan is proven wrong, and glory goes to God.

So how should we overcome temptation? Remember we're looking at the Lord's Prayer and "Lead us not into temptation. But deliver us from evil."

At the start of the book of Job, Satan accuses Job before God. It's a long story, a big discourse but you get to the end of the book and in Job 42:10 NIV is the outcome of all of that stuff that goes on between Job and the accusations and in the final outcome it says, "...the LORD restored his fortunes and gave him twice as much as he had before.."

Oh, that's not too bad, is it? The outcome wasn't too bad. Just the passage through the middle was not so good. We got to know that God might give Satan permission to tempt us. God wants you to prove to the devil that you're on God's side, that you belong to Jesus, who purchased you with his blood, that you are a blood-bought son/daughter of God that you love him from your heart out of freewill and not because of what he has done for you.

The moment you overcome temptations, something happens in the supernatural. God's name is glorified. God laughs at Satan. God is pleased with you. Jesus will be filled with joy as he intercedes for you. Blessings will come your way. God will send angels to protect you and the latter part of your life will be better than the former. You will be blessed because you overcame temptation.

All Christians should know when Satan comes and brings temptation; our loving Father has let this be. God wants us to rely on him, to rely on him for our power and strength, our wisdom, our counsel. He wants us to rely on him, but sometimes, when Satan comes along and brings temptations, we try and handle it in our own strength and that's where we have some difficulties.

Sometimes you might win. Sometimes you might lose, but you're handling it in your own strength. He wants us to rely on Him and on His strength when there is a difficulty, when there is a temptation. Temptation is not just in the form of a curvaceous young lady. All the guys look.

Temptation comes, not just in the form of a 'tempt', but temptation comes in the form of destruction. When you smash your car up and it's totally destroyed and you're lying in the hospital with dozens of broken bones and internal injuries, that's temptation. Did you know that? It might not be that serious. Let's hope it isn't, but that is temptation. We are tempted at that time to let go of God. "God, you didn't protect me. You said you would protect me and look at this. Smashed, the car is destroyed and now major financial problems, because of that, I'm hurt, in pain and I'm going to be weeks or months recovering." That's the time when the temptation comes. Temptation comes out of the destruction that Satan brings into our lives.

God did not stop Jesus from being tempted, did he? The Bible says that he was tempted in all points, like as we are. Hebrews 4:15 In all points, so if temptation comes, remember temptation came to Jesus and God allowed it, but He won against the temptation so it must be possible for us to win also.

We know that Jesus was God, but he was also human. As a human, he didn't give in to the temptation. Then it must be possible for us to not give in to the temptation. Think of some of the accusations that came against him... "That so-called son of yours will misuse your name and the authority that you've given him. He will be taken by the pleasures and treasures of this world. He will put you to the test". This is my rephrasing of the temptations that came to Jesus in the wilderness Matthew 4:1-11. God carefully listens to the accusations that Satan brings against people, against Jesus, against us and he gave Satan permission to find out for himself where Jesus belongs. Did you know that? God actually gave permission to Satan to tempt Jesus. It says in Matthew 4:1 NIV it was after Jesus' baptism. It says, "Then Jesus was led by the Spirit into the desert to be tempted by the devil." God took him into the desert for the purpose of temptation.

When I first saw that I couldn't believe it. That's pretty amazing, isn't it? God actually took him to the place of temptation. God himself can hand you over to the devil to tempt you and Satan will put you into a situation of temptation. God relies on you to prove to the devil that his accusations are wrong. God is relying on you to prove that.

Your role is very important. You have to choose where the glory is going. You choose where the glory is going. Are you going to give glory to God by overcoming the temptation or are you going to give glory to Satan by giving in to the temptation?

Satan uses all his available techniques to tempt us. He has got a basket full of them, toolbox full of them, but Jesus was firm; He wanted to please his Father. Jesus replied with, "It is written," didn't he? Every time Satan came to him, Jesus replied with, "It is written," and he gave him the word of God.

Now how can you give the word of God to Satan in the time of temptation? You have the word of God, haven't you? You can't give it if you haven't got it. If it's not in your heart and mind, it can't come out of there. If we have not put it in our heart, we're not going to get it out of our mouths. You're not going to get out what you need in the tough times if you have not put it in in the good times. We've got to plant the word into our lives so that when those tough times come, we've got something there that we can draw out and use as the strength.

In the end, Satan lost and he was filled with great shame and he ran away. It tells us in Matthew 4:11 he ran off, he couldn't take it anymore. Jesus fired the word at him. He just kept firing the word at him and it says – "and Satan left and the angels came and ministered to him."

But today Satan is putting forward accusations to God about Christians, about people you know, about you, about me. Wow, are you that important? Both Satan and God are in the discussion about you. Yes, you are, because you are a saint of God, because you are a child of God, because God honours you, because God loves you, because God blesses you, and he wants to see good in your life, he wants to see you overcoming, he wants to see you stronger and he wants to see you be the one that proves to Satan that his accusations have no grounding when it comes to you.

That's good. That's why you're important. That's why Satan comes to bring the accusations because he thinks, "I know how to get him. I know how to get her!" He knows.

When Christians give in to temptation, we give glory to Satan. But when we overcome temptation, we give glory to God. There was a lady who had done very well in business, she started out with nothing. She loved the Lord and started to take her Bible everywhere, taking it to work and always sharing with people about God.

One day, she had finished work for the day and the cash sales were good. She took the cash from her business that day and she got into the car to go home. A thief came and robbed her, snatching her bag with the takings. He opened the bag and there was the Bible, he threw the Bible back at her and ran off with the money, all her takings for the day.

She was distraught, totally distressed. She started to question everything. She went back to the church, she took her Bible to the church and left it there and thought, "God, you've not helped me. God, you go back and stay in your church. I don't want any more to do with you!" She obviously hadn't been taught how to be grounded in the Word. She thought God had blessed her and now God had left her, so she left him.

We need to have our faith fixed in God. We need to have a faith which is not shaken by negative circumstances when stuff happens, when stuff goes wrong in our life. Not long ago on my computer's screensaver, different photos we had saved came up. A photo of our son came up showing our upturned car that he had managed to creatively drive in such a manner that used the roof instead of the wheels. I encourage him to be creative but that was taking it a bit far.

We could have got really upset, but God protected him, and he got out of that car roll without a scratch even though the car was a write-off. We could have said, "God, you're supposed to protect my stuff as well as my son." But God wants us to honour him in the negative circumstances and sometimes there are negative circumstances in life. Sometimes things go wrong.

We want to see what was happening to this lady in the spiritual realm when she fell. She fell because of a temptation from Satan. The temptation was authorized by God. Satan went to God and started accusing her. "You say she loves you and that you're pleased with her. It's because of all the money that you've given her. Take the money away and see if she still loves you." That is the accusation Satan makes before God.

The robber comes in, takes away her money and she falls apart. Would she still love God without the money? She gave up. Satan was given permission and he succeeded with his temptation, showing God that this woman was on his side.

God has no way of proving to Satan that you and I will love him from the bottom of our hearts. He has no way of proving it. Only we have the way of proving this love. Only you and I have the way of proving to Satan that we love God with our whole heart, we do that when we overcome temptation. We prove it when we will not succumb to his request, his accusation that we don't love God with our whole heart; his accusation of when bad things happen, we will stop loving God.

Suppose there's a husband, faithful to his wife, a good man, then another woman starts making accusations against him. She accuses him of being with another woman, what would the wife do? Well, I'm not a woman. All I can say is what I would do. If I was the wife, then I would say, "Well, I trust my husband. Let him prove who he loves by his actions."

Now some have notably failed that test, making big news if they are a big name. But if we let people prove who they love by their actions, regardless of the circumstance, good, bad or indifferent, good, bad and ugly, we actually prove to God and to Satan that we love God with our whole heart, regardless of the difficulties that happen around us.

When we overcome temptation, God's name is glorified, we receive the supernatural power and blessing of the Holy Spirit. Our minds and our bodies may be weak, but God is telling us that he has put his word in our mouth. We have to have that word planted deep in us, so that when difficult times come, the thing that comes out of our mouth is the word of God and not, "Oh My God! Look at the circumstances," because we're then consumed by the situation that surrounds us instead of by what we've set in our heart.

Leo Harris (founder of CRC Churches International in Adelaide, Australia) used to say you can only get to keep what you can hold under pressure. When pressure comes, what you get to keep is that which you held through the pressure. When the pressure is on, we react. How are we going to react when the pressure is on?

There was a brother in tears. He had become the leader of his country and there has never been anybody with a yearning heart after God like this man. Every time he spoke, you could sense the presence of the Holy Spirit in his life. God had blessed him with everything he needed in life and then one day, he came crying with tears. This was an important situation in the nation of Israel at the time. Israel was in crisis and King David was sleeping with another man's wife.

Satan proved his accusations against David and David succumbed to the temptation. Satan had created favourable circumstances for his temptation and David failed the test. The Bible tells us that David was never the same after that.

Another sister failed. This is another true story and this couple love God so much. Regularly the man and his wife would pray, they would repent and they would offer sacrifices and they would offer sacrifices on behalf of their children in case one of them had done something wrong.

The couple's fear of God was known far and wide. This was the case of Job and his wife that I mentioned earlier. One day, after Satan's accusations, God gave Satan permission to tempt Job. He gave him permission to tempt him. What happened? Satan had the authority to tempt him, but God told him, "You can't touch his body." So, he touched everything else. Killed all his oxen, killed all his donkeys, set fire to his fields and burned his sheep. All his servants died. Job's sons and daughters were all killed and then in the second test when Satan couldn't prove it, he went back before God and said, "Ah, but if you touch his body, he will curse you."

Satan was given permission and he touched him with boils and his body was in pain and agony and his wife cursed him and said, "Why don't you just curse God and die?" because nothing else is worth living for. It was in this circumstance that Job refused to curse God.

Job refused to let his love for his God be moved even by all of that. It was too much for Mrs. Job, but it was Mr. Job who stood firm. If Mrs. Job had known that God was watching and it was a test and that He was watching to see how she performed, maybe she would have performed differently. Maybe if we realize that when we go through the difficult circumstances of life God is watching to see how we perform. He's watching to see who we will honour in those circumstances. He's watching to see who we will give glory to. Will we stand strong and resist the temptation? Will we stand strong and say, "God, I love you no matter what"?

You can be protected from the temptation; this is where we come back to this message about the Lord's Prayer where it says, "Lead me not into temptation."

See, it's the prayer. The prayer says, "I am asking, God. Don't lead me into temptation." We know that God led Jesus into temptation. We know that Satan comes and accuses the brethren before God and God gives permission for them to be tempted.

Jesus, in instructing us about prayer, says for us to pray and ask God to not give Satan permission. Satan does all kinds of stuff to us, destructive things around our life, our family, our circumstances, our possessions, our body and our health, He does those things to see if we will prove him right and God wrong, that we don't love God from the bottom of our heart because we can't love him through this.

But here, in the Lord's Prayer, Jesus teaching us to pray says, "Pray like this. Father,..." because that's who the prayer is addressed to, "Lead me not into temptation." Don't give him permission to touch me. Don't give him permission to tempt me. Don't give him permission to sift me like wheat like the disciples, because God gave him that permission.

He gave them permission in those circumstances, we know about Peter, that we read earlier, Peter came and Jesus said, "Satan has asked to sift you like wheat, (to tempt you) but!" There was a 'but' in there. "But I have prayed for you, so when you have recovered, strengthen your brothers."

Effectively He is saying, "If you pray that God doesn't let you go into temptation, you don't have to deal with that." Doctors can often cure disease, but it's always better if we don't get the disease, so we don't have to go to the doctor. Prevention is better than cure. We have a problem, we go to try and get it fixed but isn't it better to live healthily, so we don't get the problem in the first place?

This is the live healthy part of the sin equation. Don't let sin into our life. Don't let temptation into our life. How do we do that? Temptation comes because the accuser of the brethren comes and throws stuff at us, so that he can prove that we don't love God from the bottom of our heart even in adverse and difficult circumstances. If we will pray as Jesus instructed us to pray, we will experience the victory He intended for us to have. Do we believe that Jesus knew what he was talking about when he was teaching about prayer? Did he know how to pray? Did He know how we ought to pray? Then perhaps we should pay attention to what he said.

He said, "Pray like this. Lead us not into temptation, but deliver us from evil." Sometimes we're in there and the evil is present. We are saying, 'Deliver me from that Lord and don't let me go into it anymore. I don't like it and I don't want to be tempted.' Why don't we pray? "God, lead me not into temptation." We could make that a daily prayer.

When we wake up in the morning say/pray, 'Father, don't let me be tempted today. Don't give Satan permission to test my life. Give me strength to go through this day. Don't give him permission to wreck it on me.' How easy is it to say that?

Oh, that we would pray as Jesus instructed us to pray; a one sentence prayer, "Lead me not into temptation, but deliver me from evil." We can do that, can't we? We don't actually have to fight the fight. The reason we had to fight the fight was because Satan came along with all his allegations to throw at us and tried to destroy us, but we don't have to fight that fight because God has already won. God has already given us the ability to ask, 'No permission, no opportunity for Satan to touch our lives,' but we have to pray. We have to pray. Jesus said, "When you pray, pray like this."

This is not just automatic. This doesn't happen just because you want it to. This happens because you prayed and the church gets stronger because we prayed and the people, who we see in difficulties, get out of those difficulties because we pray, because we pray as Jesus said He would pray for Peter. "But I have prayed for you, so when you've recovered, strengthen your brothers," and we can pray and the thing that stops the church from being strong is this lack of prayer. One of Satan's great weapons is to stop the church praying, because we won't be effective if we don't pray, and we won't realize and take action on the power that we have.

So let us pray. Let us pray with power. Let us pray with passion. Let us pray, so that we win. Amen?

Let's pray.
Thank you God.
Father, we thank you for your word. We thank you that you've taught us to pray. Lord, we thank you that you taught us about life, you taught us the things that would help us in this life. So, Father God, we've just been talking about that little part of that prayer that you taught us. Father, we pray today that you would help us to understand, to have that revelation about your word, your word that says, "Lead us not into temptation."

Father, I pray for your people. I pray that we would understand that word, that we would receive that word, that we would embrace that word, that that word would become a part of us, that we would practise that word. Lord, that we would take hold of it and practise it and do it. Lord help us to be strong and strengthen ourselves and our lives, strengthen our families, our church and make a difference in our community because we pray and because one of things we pray is, "lead me not into temptation". Father, don't let Satan have permission to tempt me today. Father, I thank you in Jesus' name.

Lord, even as you had put that hedge of protection around Job, Father, I put that hedge of protection around each and every one reading here today.

Father, we thank you for the hedge of protection that you've given us. We receive it Father, and whatever circumstances may be unfolding in our lives, Father, the difficult ones, the evil ones, the ones that have already come into our lives that are destructive, Father, we pray that you would deliver us from evil and from the evil one. In Jesus name, amen.

7

The Doxology

I think God is awesome, don't you?
I think He's more awesome than awesome.
We've been working our way through the Lord's Prayer, we now come to the end of the Lord's Prayer.

It's an absolutely awesome ending. However, we've read from the NIV version, it's already finished in the last chapter, but if you read in the King James Version, there is what's called the Doxology or the ending to the Lord's Prayer, which is not in every translation of the Scriptures but nonetheless, it is in the King James Version.

It says in Matthew 6:13b KJV "For thine is the kingdom, and the power, and the glory forever. Amen." Wow! That's awesome. "For thine is the kingdom, and the power, and the glory" Have you been lost in the glory, lost in the worship, lost in His presence? It's fantastic! But that's nothing in comparison to the glory of God we will behold one day.

Now, it's actually not in Luke's version and it's not in some of the translations of Matthew's gospel. It's not even in some of the early manuscripts, but it has been there and there's some conjecture about whether it was part of the words that Jesus actually spoke, however, it's been in and used as part of the Lord's Prayer by most parts of the church, most of the time. And the reason that there's some conjecture about it is in the earlier manuscripts, there are ten different known endings to the Lord's Prayer. These different endings are in different translations of the Scriptures. The one I've just quoted to you is the most commonly used and the one that was adopted as the accepted one and was standardized. It's thought to have been styled on this verse in 1 Chronicles 29:11 KJV which says, "Thine, Oh Lord is the greatness, and the power, and the glory, and the victory, and the majesty. For all that is in the heaven and the earth is thine. Thine is the kingdom O Lord, and thou art exalted as head above all."

Well, it's a bit of a longer version, isn't it? But that is more or less saying the same thing. It is a doxology; it means an ending. Doxology is just a religious word. We don't need it, really. It just means an ending and it's the way in which the early church always concluded its prayers, with a doxology, like a recognized ending. We usually say Amen, that's our ending. That's our doxology. The early church had this recognition of the awesomeness of God as part of its ending of its prayers.

Some think that the reason it's not recorded in some of the versions is simply because the doxology was so obvious that everybody did it, it didn't need to be written down. I don't know whether that's true or not but that thought is out there, that perhaps, in some of the versions where it's not recorded, that was the reason.

The doxology was so obvious, that it was not necessary to write it down.

In fact, today, 2000 years on, many parts of the church still have formal doxologies in their service, in their prayers and at the end of the service. The way in which they conclude the service is to say the doxology. I've been in lots of churches where they say the doxology, which is signifying, this is the end of the service. That's really all it means and we're giving glory and recognition to God. However, this is an awesome doxology, "For thine is the kingdom, and the power, and the glory forever."

Let's look at what it says. "Thine is the kingdom" I'm pretty excited about that because Jesus' whole life and ministry was about the kingdom. He taught about the kingdom. He told so many parables, saying; "the kingdom of God is like" ... "the kingdom of God is like a farmer who went out to sow". It's like the man who lost a pearl. He told all these stories because He was trying to convey to the people what the kingdom of God is like.

As we looked at that earlier, when we read about "Your Kingdom come," we found that the kingdom of God is like God invading our life. It's like God taking over every part of our lives. The whole purpose of the Lord's Prayer is in fact, that we might understand that God wants to be in every part of our lives.

"Thine is the kingdom." Jesus taught mostly about the kingdom. He related about the kingdom being all parts of life. The kingdom of God is about me, it's about my life and it being centred in God. That's what the kingdom of God is all about. It's an acknowledgement that all of life comes from God and flows back to God. That's what the kingdom is about. Jesus said, "The kingdom is near to you." And then to others He said, "The kingdom is within you."

He's talking about the kingdom. The kingdom is about our life exalting God. It's about God invading every part of our life, not just Sunday. God is interested in being involved in every part of our life. He is Life.

He is the kingdom. It's not that God has got this thing on His side called the kingdom. He is the kingdom. When we are worshipping God, we're exalting the kingdom, but we should be exalting God by worshipping Him through every part of our day, through every activity, in every part of our week and every part of our life, not just on a Sunday morning sing-along.

Any part of our life that is not centred in Him will be done away with. Think about that one. Apostle Paul wrote in 1 Corinthians 3:11-13 NIV "For no man can lay a foundation other than the one which is laid, which is Jesus Christ. Now if any man builds on the foundation with gold, silver, precious stones, wood, hay, straw, each man's work will become evident; for the day will show it because it is *to be* revealed with fire, and the fire itself will test the quality of each man's work."

Wow! What happens to gold in the fire? It melts and it purifies. What happens to wood in the fire? It burns and it turns into a bit of charcoal. What happens to straw in the fire? It's gone. It's totally disintegrated. What he's saying here is; you can build your life however you like. You can build your life with whatever you like but your life will be tested by the fire of God.

How much of your life will be left after it's tested by the fire of God? Will your life be built with gold, silver, and precious stones, things that are not consumed but only purified? or, will it be built with wood, hay and straw, things that are burned up and consumed and there's nothing left? That's what the kingdom is about, building our life out of things that are permanent, building our life out of things that have eternal value.

We are here to acknowledge His kingdom. That's what we're here for. We're here to proclaim His kingdom. We're here to live in His kingdom. We're here to establish His kingdom and we're here until He comes to reign in His kingdom. That's what we're here for. So that's the kingdom. "For thine is the kingdom."

"And the power." Jesus demonstrated the power of God, didn't he? He demonstrated the power of God by his life. The kingdom of God is a higher kingdom. It's on a higher plane than the kingdoms of this world. Mankind builds his kingdoms, but they come and they go. Some have built great kingdoms that have lasted generations, even hundreds of years or more, but they're gone. Great empires have been raised up that have lasted even a thousand years or more, but they're gone.

But the kingdom of God goes on. The kingdom is demonstrated. Jesus demonstrated it by healing the sick. He showed that He was here to take us to a higher plane. When we can't heal the sick, Jesus did. He demonstrated the kingdom by raising the dead; He took us to a higher level.

We can't do anything about the dead. Once they've gone that's it, but Jesus raised them back to life on several occasions. He cast out demons. Humans can't do that, but Jesus did because he had authority in a higher plane. Demons belong to a spiritual plane, Jesus had authority in that spiritual plane therefore He cast out the demons.

He changed the elements of the world, changed the water into wine. Have you done that? No? Have you walked on water? It wasn't a frozen lake, incidentally. You might have walked on water when it's frozen, but have you walked on a wet lake? Jesus did that. He took authority over the elements of the earth. He changed the weather, speaking to the storm and saying, "Be still" and instantly it calmed.

Jesus had authority over all these things, supernaturally multiplying the elements. He fed the five thousand with just five loaves of bread and two fish, and the leftovers taken up was twelve basketful. At the end there was more than what they had started with! It says they fed five thousand men PLUS women and children. So altogether there was probably a crowd of between fifteen to twenty thousand people and he fed them all with five loaves and two fish, finishing the meal with more than they had started with. Isn't God awesome? He's on a different plane to what we're on. He, Jesus, resurrected from the dead. Wow! That's kind of pretty awesome.

That's power; God said that the same spirit that raised Jesus from the dead would live in us, that some of us might be raised from the dead. I have met people, maybe you have, that have been raised from the dead. Pastor Emmanuel Twagiriimana from Nairobi, Kenya, Africa; (I have stayed at his home a couple of times) Ps Bill from Fiji, a pastor I met at an Indian pastors training seminar, raised from the dead. I've met other people that have been raised from the dead like Matt an Aussie who came on mission with us to

East Africa, three times died and on three separate occasions raised from the dead. That's awesome.

This is in God's realm. It's not in our plane, it's not in the realms that we live as human beings, but people being raised from the dead happens. It happens when God comes and invades people's lives. Jesus also had a teaching that was above the plane of human teaching, philosophy and knowledge. He taught about and he showed by example; love, acceptance, and forgiveness. That's not on the human plane. What he showed was beyond the human realm.

There's an awesome amount of power in love. There's an awesome amount of power in acceptance, accepting someone for who they are, not necessarily for what they've done. Yes, you're a person, I accept you. You may have done something awesomely great, or you may have done something disastrously bad, I accept you because you're a person.

We've talked about forgiveness earlier. The power of forgiveness sets people free, but Jesus didn't just talk about it, he didn't just command people to do it, he actually did it. On the cross he said, "Father, forgive them. They don't know what they're doing." He demonstrated everything that he taught. He demonstrated the kingdom by bringing the kingdom and invading our sphere, by invading earth with the power of the kingdom.

It's not about acknowledging some spiritual supremacy. Church is not about that; it's about seeing a practical outworking of the message of Jesus in our lives. Some parts of the church would teach that it's just about the supremacy of Christ and it's all theological and it doesn't actually invade our space. It doesn't actually make a difference in our practical, tangible world in which we live, but Jesus did. Jesus did make a difference in the practical and tangible world in which He lived. He brought the kingdom of God in power.

When Apostle Paul preached the Gospel he said, "I didn't come to you in the power of fancy words. I came to you in the demonstration of the Gospel and the power of God" 1 Corinthians 2.4 (My paraphrase). God is at work in our lives if we will let Him be. Are we letting Him be at work in our lives? He wants to do the things that are practical and real and tangible in our lives because that's the power of God.

We have seen so often, the power of God touch and heal people, setting them free from demonic power and free from physical problems in their lives. Jesus said that we would do what He did. Think about this, here are a few quotes from Jesus. He said, "... you will do the same things that I am doing. You will do even greater things, now that I am going back to the Father." John 14.12 CEV

He said, "they will lay hands on the sick, and they will recover." Mark 16:18 NKJ He said, "And these signs will follow those who believe:" Mark 16:17 NKJV He said, "Have faith in God (literally have the faith of God). For assuredly, I say to you, whoever says to this mountain, 'Be removed and be cast into the sea,' and does not doubt in his heart, but believes that those things he says will be done, he will have whatever he says ."Mark 11:22-23 NKJV

He said, "I have given to you authority to trample on snakes and scorpions and over all the power of the enemy and nothing will by any means, harm you." Luke 10:19 NIV

That's what Jesus said. I think that's practical. I don't think that it's just about some spiritual supremacy that we are created to be more like God and will one day be like him. Yes, we will one day be like him, and we are growing in that right now, but it's all about that practical outworking of a kingdom in our lives. God is calling us to be the demonstration of the power of God, to be the demonstration of the kingdom of God right here.

I was talking to Pastor Ric Burrell of Strong Nation Church, Hawkesbury, N.S.W., Australia; he said something, and I thought, "That's just awesome." He was telling me about how he views the church that he pastors, and he said, "Church is like a motor mechanic's workshop. You bring your car to a motor mechanic and get your tyres checked, and get your engines serviced, you get a few loose nuts tightened up, and you get a few damaged and worn out parts replaced, and it's all set up and ready to go again, to go out into the world and be a motorcar." He said, "I feel like I'm the mechanic. I'm not the minister of the church, the people are the ministers of the church, and I'm the mechanic that fixes up the ministers so they can go and minister."

I thought, it is just so good that my job is not just to do the ministry. My job is to make sure that the ministers i.e. the members of the congregation, are ready and prepared to go and do the ministry. We just need to go out into the world and be the kingdom. It's not something we've got to do, it's not something that's put on us; we just have to be. We just have to know who we are, be and demonstrate the kingdom in our lives.

The apostles, prophets, pastors, teachers and evangelists are the ones who prepare the church to go and be the ministers of the kingdom. We can and still should see, the power of God at work in the church service, but that shouldn't be the only place we see the kingdom of God at work. The kingdom of God should be so at work in us as believers, that we go out from our church meetings well equipped to be who we are meant to be and we demonstrate the Kingdom of God in our community, in our family, in our work, in all the places that we go, in the shops that we visit. We demonstrate the power of God just simply by being, because we are; therefore, be. Hallelujah. The power of God is awesome, isn't it? The greatness of God is awesome. The presence of God is awesome and we just sense and know the presence of God is where the power of God is.

If we would seek after that presence, we would find that power because the power of God is in His presence. So often, we come, we want a religious experience, we go to church as a duty, as an obligation, (this is my habit) and we don't seek after His presence, but we need to seek after his presence. Seeking after His presence is where we find His power. It's not just to have the power in my life, but to let the power flow through my life.

The scripture says, "For thine is the kingdom and the power." We just looked at some of the examples of the power that Jesus portrayed to us, changing the elements, healing the sick and raising the dead, etc. That same power, the same power that Jesus has, the same power that Jesus demonstrates, is at work in us. It's not that He is different; because John said "because as He is, so are we in this world." 1 John 4:17 NKJV

He's given to us his righteousness, 2 Corinthians 5:21 it's not as though He was more righteous than we are. We are human and we have sinned, and we fall short, but He has prepared us and shown us forgiveness saying "I'm going to bring you into my presence. I'm going to bring you to be like me so that when you are like me, you can do what I do." Jesus said, "I love the Father and do exactly what my Father has commanded me." John 14.31 NIV he was the demonstration of the Father.

When we look at Jesus, we see what the Father is, but we also see what we are. When we look in the scriptures and we see how Jesus is, we also see how we are, but then our mind takes over. Oops! Our mind takes over and sees us how we see ourselves from a human, fleshly, worldly perspective. We don't see ourselves as Jesus sees us and how He says WE ARE.

We see ourselves from a human perspective, we see ourselves with our weaknesses and with our shortcomings, we see ourselves with our failings and our ailments and the things that stop us from being Jesus; but Jesus doesn't see us like that. He sees us how He's made us. He's made us like Him. Amen?

Let the power of God touch you right now. Right where you are, just let the power of God touch you. As we seek after Him, let the power of God just touch you right now. Right now. You might have a need; physical, mental, emotional, financial. You might have a need, but let the awesome presence of God touch you and let that power of God that's in you, touch you now. Thank you, Jesus. Thank you, Jesus. Thank you, Jesus. Just let the power of God touch you right now. For a few moments just close your eyes, focus on Jesus. Just let what He's done, be seen in you right now.

Let me pray for you:
PRAYER
Father, I thank you for the power of God present in the person reading this. I thank you for your power, Lord to touch them, to

heal and to set them free in every way. Thank you, Father, that as they reach out to you, your power is there to touch and change their life, influence their life and cause them to be the demonstration of your glory and your power in the earth today. Thank you, my God.

The Glory.
For thine is the kingdom and the power, and the glory. The glory that's felt in worship in the singing, in shouting, in laughter, in listening, in silence. Amazing. It's such contrast. The glory is heard in prophetic word and song. My dad physically heard the angels singing one night. That was his encounter with God.

The glory is seen in healing. The glory is seen in supernatural manifestations, I've seen so many and heard many others, about gold dust touching people, settling on their hands and face, (it happened to me), teeth being filled with gold or silver, about people falling over in the power of God. Laughter, I've seen halos on people, the whole body glows because the glory of the presence of God is there. We can sometimes see the presence of God.

It's not contrived, it's not rehearsed, we've not prepared for it. You can't practise it. You have to practise the presence when you're in the presence, the glory is there, it comes when we prepare our hearts in prayer. It comes as we pursue him with the passion and as we press in until we touch him with the same passion as the woman with the issue of blood. She pressed through the crowd. She was determined. We have to have that same kind of determination. We're going to press through and touch the hem of His garment, and then we will come into His presence and see the glory. We'll feel the glory. We will demonstrate the glory and power of God to others both now and forever and ever.

Luke 1:33 KJV says that the angels prophesied to Mary about the child that she would bear, and they said, "And he shall reign over the house of Jacob forever and of His kingdom there shall be no end." Exodus 15:18 KJV said, "Then the Lord shall reign forever and ever." And the Psalm 146:10 KJV says, "The Lord shall reign forever, even thy God, O Zion, to all generations. Praise ye the Lord!

And the book finishes in Revelation 11:15 NKJV with "And the seventh angel sounded," the last of seven. "Then the seventh angel sounded: And there were loud voices in heaven, saying, "The kingdoms of this world have become *the kingdoms* of our Lord and of His Christ, and He shall reign forever and ever!"

How great is our God?
Seek His presence.
Worship in His glory.
Demonstrate His power.

Bibliography

In His Presence,
EW Kenyon, Kenyon's Gospel Publishing Society Inc, Seattle, Washington, USA 1944

Anything you ask in My name I will do, so that the Father may be glorified in the Son.
Colin Urquhart, Hodder & Stoughton, Seven Oaks, Kent, UK 1978

Overcoming Satan in One Short Sentence,
Makko Musagarra, Trinity Printing and Publishers, Kampala, Uganda.

The Plain Man looks at the Lord's Prayer,
William Barclay, Collins- Fontana Books, UK, 1964

Heavenly Man,
Brother Yun, co-written and translated by Paul Hattaway, Zondervan, Nashville, TN. USA 2008.

What Australian Christian Leaders are saying

"As you read Your Kingdom Come, A Different Way to Look at the Lord's Prayer you will be inspired by Howard's very practical and in-depth look at our Lord's prayer. Though it could easily be called Our Prayer, Howard's unpacking of The Lord's Prayer is a great insight into how a Christian's life was intended to be lived within God's Kingdom; and when it is, that life impacts all lives around it. This book is likely to challenge you, and I pray it will take you on a life-long journey of walking in His Kingdom."

Pastor Ric Burrell

Snr Ps Strong Nation Church, Hawkesbury, Penrith, Blue Mountains NSW Australia & Cambodia.

District leader, Australian Christian Churches.

"From his opening citation of Clyde Herring's witty, amusing, and provocative expansion of The Lord's Prayer, Dr Sands goes on to dig deeply into the true meaning and application of what it means to pray as Jesus taught us. His book provides an excellent analysis of the structure and terms used in the prayer, but far more, every page is redolent of the author's deep devotion to Christ and of a strong relationship with the Lord. Your Kingdom Come could be read as an extended devotional, perhaps a chapter a day, mixed with prayer and serious meditation. For slower readers, perhaps *only a portion of a chapter, depending upon how much time is available. But anyone who reads this book thoughtfully, and with a mind open to the Holy Spirit, will, in my opinion, be enriched by the encounter."*

Rev Dr Ken Chant BA, MRE, DMin, ThD, PhD,
Member of the Order of Australia.
Ordained in the CRC Churches International (since 1954).
Ministry: Founder, with Dr Stan DeKoven of the worldwide Vision Christian College, and Australasian president of the same.
Vision College, founded in 1974, currently has some 100,000 students in about 150 countries, with about 2 million graduates, who have established more than 10,000 new churches.

"What a well of refreshing and inspiration read from the Lord's Prayer by Howard Sands. During our season of over 30 years ministry in Papua New Guinea, the believers never knew God as God, but it was always "Papa God" or Father God.

I loved those early chapters. I thought here in the Lord's prayer we have the complete Gospel message for mankind, especially believers. Not some ritual or something spoken during a church service but the complete whole message in 5 verses."

Rev Dr Graham Baker DD MA
Missionaries to PNG 1965-96 (Together with Dr Irene Baker)
Missions Director for the Foursquare Churches 1997-2016, 19
Director of Lighthouse Global Ministries 1996-

"Most of us can recite the Lord's Prayer rote without thinking about what it means. Howard has opened this gem of a prayer and shown us what Jesus meant when He told us to pray it. There are lots of good thoughts here which can open new doors in your thinking, and introduce you to some new and exciting vistas for your faith."

Pastor Tony Rawson
Evangelist and conference speaker
CRC Churches International.

"Thank you, Howard, for this insightful, relevant, and practical book. It will certainly help to encourage and revitalize the lives of those who read it. Your reflections on the Lord's Prayer and truths about the kingdom of God are obviously the result of much thought and many years of effective ministry experience throughout the world.

In these times of darkness, when the kingdoms this world are being shaken, when the truth is being so severely challenged, and the spirit of fear is destroying so many lives, we need to be reminded of the unshakeable nature of the kingdom of God. Your book does this, and importantly helps us to know how to pray effectively and how to be relevant, faithful, and powerful ambassadors of God's kingdom."

Pastor Richard Kerridge
Perth, WA, Australia
Liberty World Missions Ltd -- Director
Associated Christian Ministers International (ACMI) –
International Chairman
Liberty Bible College – Principal
Africa Business Community (ABC) - Director

"This book gives a true understanding of what we call the Lords Prayer, giving a biblical meaning to this amazing scripture, explaining true Christianity as a relationship with God. Discounting the law as only a shadow of what God really has for us. Understanding and revelation will be received from reading this manuscript, well done!"

Ps John Gear
International Network of Churches
Chairman, Blacktown Ministers Network.

"This challenging and practical walk-through of the Jesus' model prayer hits at the heart of the daily life of a follower of Christ. It's message is an encouragement and a paradigm shift to believers of all stages. This is exactly what Howard has demonstrated over decades of faithful, humble service to our Lord in Australia and beyond. I commend Howard, his ministry and this book to you."

Pastor Darren Hessenberger
Senior Pastor,
Highlands Christian Church, Mittagong, Australia
International Missions Coordinator, Bethesda Ministries International

"This short book on the Lord's Prayer is written with the clear intention of opening up the Prayer for everyday use. Both readers who have prayed the Prayer for decades and those who have never prayed it will find this book equally thought-provoking, engaging and inviting. Howard speaks from his heart and this work reflects his own personal love for our Father in heaven of whom he writes."

Rev Dr Barry Chant BA, BD, DMin, PhD, DipEd
Author and Teacher
Founding President, Tabor College Australia

"This Book is so important for every believer to read! A Prayerless believer is a powerless believer. Oh how we need to get back into the prayer closet every day! Howard Sands has released this book in a crucial time, and hopefully this will be a wake-up call to many, to return to the Lord as their first Love & get on their knees in prayer!"

Pastor Matt Prater – New Hope Church, Brisbane, Australia
Host– Historymakers radio & Vision radio Weekends presenter
Former Chairman – National Day of Prayer & Fasting Australia

Other Books By Howard Sands

The Foundations

The Foundations delivers transforming lessons for the Christian believer (especially suited for new believers) to build strong "The Foundations" of their Christian faith. The book is divided into 10 easy to follow lessons, each including 10 enlightening discussion questions. They help you clearly understand and establish the vital foundations of the Christian faith to become a true disciple of Jesus Christ.

Developed from a pastors perspective, to strengthen new believers into powerful disciples of Jesus, who understand from the very beginning who they are in Christ and how to live victoriously in Him. During his own pastoring and discipling of new believers, Howard was aware of a shortage of material that adequately dealt with this and began writing material to use in his church. This material has now been proven over many years in establishing new Christians, it has been improved and refined over the years to provide this powerfully succinct book you have today.

Ideal for:- Churches new Christian classes, One on one discipleship, Individual studies for new Christians Refreshing those older in the faith in their reason for believing.

Crusade - Seminar Manual

This crusade - seminar manual came about through working with several strong church planting movements in India between 1979 and 2000 and observing their preparations, actions and omissions. We wrote the manual to help those leaders see collectively what they and several other organisations were doing that provided great results for the kingdom of God and caused new churches to be planted and existing ones to grow by the new salvations recorded at the crusades and then by their families and connections.

So in reality this is the collect wisdom of those organisations, my observations and then their applications of my instructions, refined over several years until we first published this work just for their use in 2000 and continued to refine it until the present. It contains some aspects that may be culturally or physically challenging for some people, all the aspects included however have been tried and proven and if you are prepared to launch out by faith and follow this manual, you and the churches that work with you will be blessed beyond measure in your outreach to win souls, all that remains for you to do is the prayer and preparation in faith along with your speakers, worship teams and hosts for a great event.

Through these principles and practices we have seen thousands of people won to Jesus Christ in several countries.

Preparing the Whole Man, To Take the Whole Gospel, To the Whole World.

https://allauthor.com/author/howardsands/

Understanding the Whole Man: Spirit Soul and Body,
Kindle Edition

This study looks at why we are here, What is God's ultimate eternal purpose and how will it be fulfilled through his perfect creation –man. It examines the fall and its effects and redemption and its purposes on each aspect of man, spirit. soul and body.

It is designed to help you understand and distinguish the faculties of your spirit. soul and body and shows how you can use them as God intended.

You will learn that God desires a family who will love Him from a free will.

You will learn how to live by the spirit instead of the soul, understanding what the sin appetites of each are and how to deal with them.

https://allauthor.com/author/howardsands/

About the Author, Howard Sands

Rev Dr Howard Sands is the founder and international director of Beautiful Feet Task Force. (BFTF)

He began the organisation in 1980 with a burning desire to both win souls and encourage the church to be active overcomers in everyday life, fulfilling the Great Commission. Born on the Scripture found in Romans 10.15, "How beautiful upon the mountains are the feet of them that bring good news ..." BFTF is based soundly on the Bible as the Word of God, historically correct, spiritually powerful and relevant for today. He believes that outside of Christ man is eternally lost and that Christ's substitutionary and sacrificial death on the cross of Calvary is the only way which man can find peace with God and eternal life; it is therefore necessary that this gospel be preached to all men, everywhere.

Howard graduated from Life Ministry Bible College, Melbourne in 1976. He founded BFTF whilst on the ministry team of the Christian Convention Centre at Mildura, Victoria, Australia in 1980. He has been, salesman, sales manager, branch manager and managing director of various business enterprises, he earned an honours certificate stage 2 from the Life Underwriters Association of Australia in 1987, he completed his Bachelor of Business with majors in Business Management and Marketing in 1994 and received the Advanced Diploma in Christian Ministry from Hope College Gold Coast in 2000 and was awarded an honorary Doctor of Divinity for 35 years of missionary service in 2014 from Good News International University in Chennai, India.

BFTF is currently involved in evangelism and leadership training in Asia and Africa. Howard has taken many small teams of leaders there to minister in evangelistic crusades, leadership conferences and church planting seminars. He has ministered in churches across Australia, India, Sri Lanka, Indonesia, UK, USA, Hong Kong, Fiji, New Zealand, Romania, Uganda, Kenya, Tanzania, Burundi, Ghana, Togo, Benin, Nigeria, Cameroon, Malawi, Zambia, South Africa, United Arab Emirates, Singapore, China and Malaysia.

Howard believes that the most effective ministry is achieved both in and sent out from the local church. Howard has been a minister with the Assemblies of God in NSW Australia since 1993.

Howard & his wife Joy were the founders/senior pastors of Canberra New Life Centre, AOG. He was a lecturer & founding board member of the Canberra Ministry Training College a multi denominational ministry training college (now Unity College). They were active at Riverlands Christian Church, Penrith NSW for over 11 years where Howard was the Missions Director and board member, Joy was the district pastors PA. For 5 years they pioneered and pastored New Life Church in Sydney's north west.

Howard now concentrates his efforts on the BFTF missions program, which includes evangelism, pastors and leadership training and visits to churches to encourage, teach and provide skills to lift people from they are in their experience to where God says they are in His word. He visits many developing world countries to develop leadership and administers the on-line platform Africa Network BFTF of over 4,000 leaders concerned for the Gospel in Africa.

Howard is married to Joy, they live in the Blue Mountains of New South Wales, Australia, they have 2 grown children and 6 grandchildren where they enjoy family get togethers and exploring bush trails with their grandchildren.